Dedicated to the memory of Mr. Richard Brandt, Spanish-American-War veteran from Baraboo, Wisconsin, who introduced F. D. Bloss to the magical world of chess.

—And to the Pulaski Chess Club of Pulaski, Virginia, which has, with great success, done this for so many young people.

Manufactured in the United States of America
ISBN 0-936015-61-6

CONTENTS

OTHER BOOKS BY F. D. BLOSS

Chess

Chess at a glance (Van Nostrand Reinhold, 1967)

Rate your own chess (Van Nostrand Reinhold, 1972)

Rate your own chess (Revised, Van Nostrand Reinhold, 1981)

Crystallography

Introduction to the methods of optical crystallography (Holt, Rinehart and Winston, 1961)

X-ray diffraction tables (Southern Illinois University Press, 1966) with J. H. Fang

Cristalografía óptica (Ediciones Omega, S.A. Barcelona, 1970)

Crystallography and crystal chemistry (Holt, Rinehart and Winston, 1971)

Laboratory manual for optical crystallography (Burgess Publishing Co., 1980) with Norris W. Jones

The spindle stage: Principles and practice (Cambridge University Press, 1981)

Crystallography and crystal chemistry (Revised, Mineralogical Society of America, 1994)

OPENING REMARKS

Despite Shelly Fischman's whimsical cartoons, which contribute much to the light-hearted flavor of the book, this book represents a serious attempt to teach chess with clarity. As a further nod to the absolute beginner, we have used three-dimensional representations of the board instead of the standard two-dimensional diagrams favored by most chess books. And by teaching chess through conversations between fish, we achieved the freedom of being able to repeat important points for emphasis. For example, one of the fish can say, "Sammy, I know you have already explained the difference between a fork and a skewer, but can you go over it again?"

We wish to thank Margie Sentelle for transforming a handwritten manuscript into the final form shown here. We also thank Ron Wirgart, Sharon Chiang and Jonathan Kensler for their help in creating earlier versions of the illustrations. Scott Mutchler and Walter Zicko offered helpful suggestions. We greatly appreciate Shelly Fischman's interest in the book and his going to the National Aquarium to make sure that the behind-the-scenes view of Sammy's tank was actually authentic. Mike Lovins of Carter Printing was a tower of strength.

We are grateful to Dr. Jim Glanville, who provided a seasoned expert's viewpoint, and to Jonathan Kensler, who provided a 12-year-old's viewpoint. Al Lawrence offered important suggestions that improved the book. Dr. Susan Eriksson provided the opinion of an adult who wished to learn chess. We thank G.V. Gibbs for being G.V. Gibbs.

F.D.B. and A.K.

Figure 1. Day after day Sammy Seahorse watched closely as two workers played chess in front of the tank he shared with Stella Starfish, Cary Grunt (narrow stripes), Gary Grouper, and Joan Crawfish (large claws).

HOW DID IT HAPPEN?

Some things cannot be explained. For example, how did Sammy the Seahorse learn to play chess? As we recall, it was because two workers at the National Aquarium in Washington, D.C., day after day, played chess in front of the tank Sammy shared with four other fish—Gary Grouper, Stella Starfish, Cary Grunt, and Joan Crawfish. And that raises another question. How could Joan, a crayfish that ordinarily lives in fresh water, survive in the saltwater of the tank she shared with the others? But never mind, she was a tough old girl, and she did.

As Sammy once explained it to us in his gurgly voice, he had learned chess by closely watching the workmen as they moved their chessmen, nicely carved from stone, across their stone chessboard (Fig. 1). Besides, he seemed to be a born chess player. Not many seahorses are.

SAMMY SEAHORSE—A member of a group of fish characterized by a horse-like head and a tail which, like a monkey's, can be wrapped around things to grasp them (= prehensile). Being slow swimmers, seahorses usually coil their tails around strands of seaweed, remaining anchored there while hiding. Studies of their sounds suggest an ability to communicate with each other. But Sammy is unique. He seems to be the only one to have mastered human speech. Sammy also used the seahorses' sharp eyesight to learn chess by watching the games in front of his tank. Indeed, by eavesdropping on the conversations between the two members of the U.S. Chess Federation who played there, he learned a great deal about the literature and lore of chess.

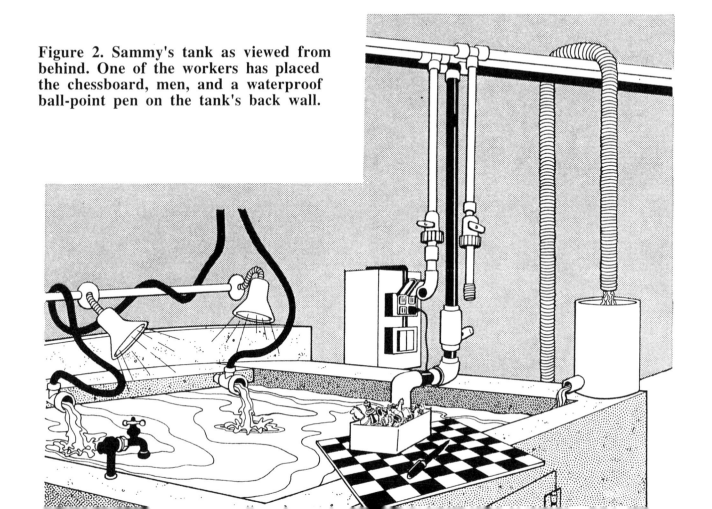

Figure 2. Sammy's tank as viewed from behind. One of the workers has placed the chessboard, men, and a waterproof ball-point pen on the tank's back wall.

While working behind the scenes to feed the fish, one worker unwisely placed the chessboard, the chessmen, and a ball-point pen on top of the back wall of Sammy's tank (Fig. 2). And another accidentally knocked it into the tank. Luckily, Sammy and his friends were at the other end of the tank, so no one was hurt as the stone chessmen and board plummeted to the bottom of Sammy's tank. The chessmen fell in a jumble at the back corner of the tank, but the chessboard landed face-up near the front of the tank.

We have tried to write this story just as Sammy told it to us. And, as friends of Sammy, we have faithfully followed Sammy's directions for drawing the illustrations for his story. Since Sammy proved to be a natural-born teacher of chess, we think you will find that Sammy's lessons and illustrations will teach you to play chess as rapidly as they did his friends Joan

CARY GRUNT—A member of a large family of fish, the grunts, which can make grunting noises by grinding their teeth. If a cloth is placed between the teeth of a living grunt, it can no longer produce the noise. The grunting noises, although not as loud as those emitted by tennis players, interfered with the subsurface listening devices of World War II submarines.

GARY GROUPER—Groupers are members of the huge sea bass family. Some types may weigh only two pounds but others reach 760 pounds. They live in warm seas and seem to be almost always hungry. Their natural food includes other fish, shrimp and crabs. Fortunately, Gary is small and always too well fed to look upon his tank mates as snacks.

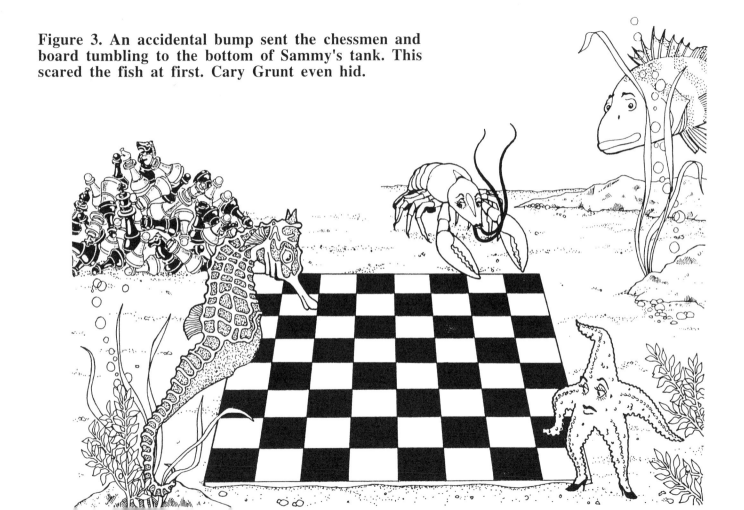

Figure 3. An accidental bump sent the chessmen and board tumbling to the bottom of Sammy's tank. This scared the fish at first. Cary Grunt even hid.

Crawfish, Cary Grunt, Gary Grouper, and Stella Starfish. Let's start.

WHITE, BLACK, AND
PLACING THE BOARD

As Sammy looked at the chessboard and the jumble of chessmen on the bottom of his tank (Fig. 3), he said to his friends, "I believe that I can play this game called chess and even teach the four of you." He then began their lesson by saying, "In chess the lighter-colored chessmen and chessboard squares are called White regardless of their actual color. And the darker men and squares are called Black, again regardless of their color.

"The Player moving the white chessmen is always called WHITE and the one moving the darker chessmen is always called BLACK. When playing, WHITE and BLACK face each other with the chessboard placed between them. The board must be placed, and this is very important, so that a white corner square is to each Player's right. Tell you what, I'll get on one side of the board and pretend to be WHITE, and the four of you can get on the opposite side and pretend to be BLACK. Note that a white corner square is to my right and the other white corner square is to your right" (Fig. 4).

PLACING THE BOARD—To your far right, a corner white.

JOAN CRAWFISH—A freshwater crayfish resembling (but smaller than) a lobster. Miraculously, Joan has thrived in the saltwater of Sammy's tank. In this she resembles her saltwater relatives, the spiny lobsters, which flourish along the coasts of Maine and Florida.

Figure 4. Sammy plays as WHITE. Gary Grouper, Cary Grunt (striped), Stella Starfish and Joan Crawfish will, together, play as BLACK. A white corner square has to be to each player's right.

BLACK

WHITE

FILES, RANKS, AND NAMING THE SQUARES (ALBEBRAIC NOTATION)

"In order for you to understand how chess players describe the way chessmen move," continued Sammy, "you'll have to use your imagination. First, imagine that we have cut the chessboard into eight long pieces, each stretching from you to me. These are called **files**. In particular, from left to right, they are called the a-, b-, c-, d-, e-, f-, g-, and h-files (Fig. 5).

Figure 5. The board divided into eight files.

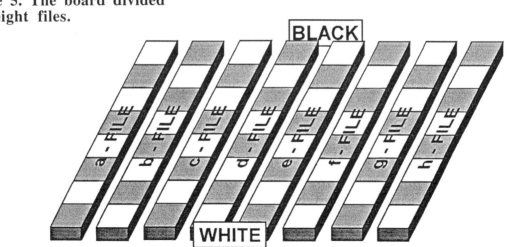

"Next imagine that the board has been cut into eight pieces perpendicular to the files. These are called **ranks** (Fig. 6). The one nearest to WHITE is called rank 1; the next, rank 2 ... and the rank farthest from WHITE (but closest to BLACK) is called rank 8."

Figure 6. The board divided into eight ranks.

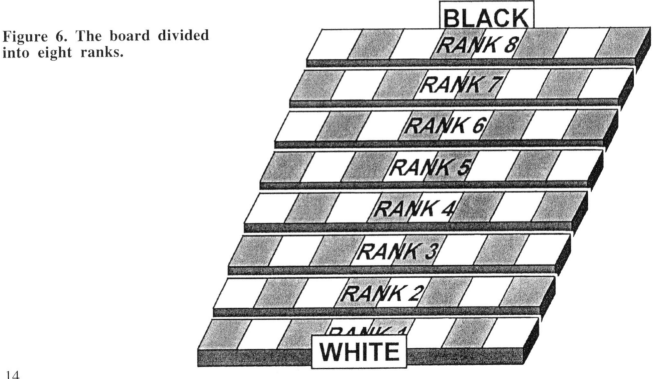

"Chess players use the **algebraic notation** to name each square of the chessboard according to the file and rank to which it belongs. To make it easier for you, I'll label each square of our chessboard with its name." Having said this, Sammy grasped the ball-point pen with his prehensile tail and properly labeled each square (Fig. 7).

Figure 7. The board with each square labeled according to the algebraic notation.

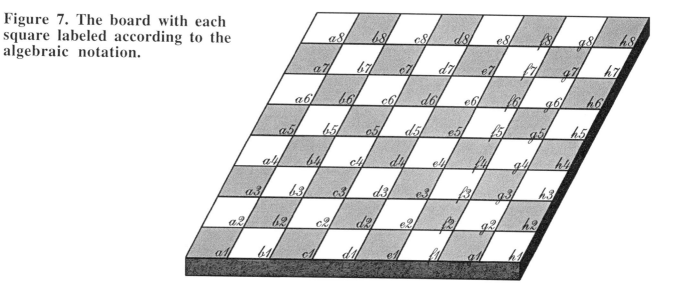

THE CHESSMEN AND THEIR MOVES
The King

"When a game begins," Sammy lectured, "each Player has an army of 16 men, one being the King. And each army battles to capture the other army's King. If you capture the enemy King, you win the game. It's easy to recognize the King. He's the tallest of all the chessmen and has a kind of cross on top. A King can move only one square at a time in any direction. Near the center of the board, a King has as many as eight squares to move to, and I'll mark each of these eight squares with an *x*" (Fig. 8).

Figure 8. Each square to which a King on d5 can move has been marked with an *x*.

The Pawns

"Each King's army includes eight Pawns. These are the shortest and, at the beginning of a game, the least valuable of all the chessmen. A Pawn can only move straight ahead in its file. For its *very first move*, a Player can choose to move a Pawn either *one square or two squares* straight ahead (Fig. 9). But after a Pawn's first move, it can only move one square at a time. And when I say straight ahead, I mean that WHITE's Pawns can move only toward BLACK, and BLACK's Pawns can only move toward WHITE. They can never move backward."

Figure 9. The Pawns in their starting positions. At its first move each can move either one or two squares forward (as illustrated for the e-Pawns).

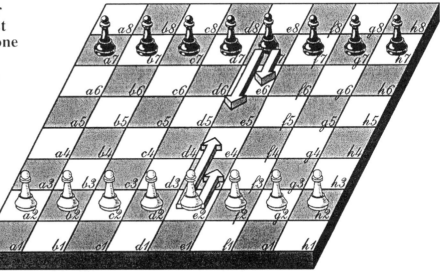

17

The Rook

Sammy, using his tail, cleared the board of chessmen and placed on it a chessman that looked like the top of a castle's tower. "This," he said, "is called a Rook. It is a powerful chessman that, given the chance, can do a lot of damage to the enemy army. It has a long reach because, if not blocked by other chessmen, it can move to any square of the rank or file it occupies. To show you, I'll draw an *x* on each of the squares to which the White Rook on b6 can

Figure 10. A Rook can move onto any square in the file or rank it occupies.

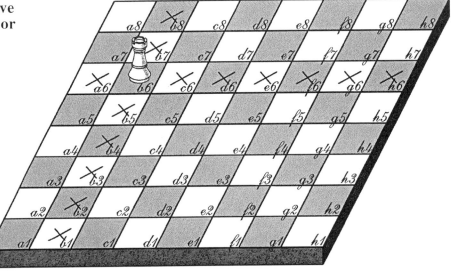

move (Fig. 10). As you can see, a Rook can move as far as desired—unless one of its own men blocks it. In such case, as I'll show for the Black Rook, it must stop short of any square occupied by its own man" (Fig. 11).

"But what if an enemy chessman occupies a square on the Rook's rank or file?" asked Joan Crawfish.

Figure 11. Because it is blocked by its own men, the Black Rook can only move onto one of the four squares marked *x*.

"Good question," said Sammy. "In that case the Rook can move onto the square occupied by the enemy chessman and remove it from the board. The Rook has captured the enemy chessman. That's the way all captures, *except by*

Pawns, are made in chess. Using its legal move, the chessman moves onto the enemy-occupied square and captures the enemy chessman. All captured chessmen are, of course, removed from the board" (Fig. 12).

Figure 12. The Black Rook can move onto any of the squares marked *x*. A White Pawn occupies one of these squares (h5) and the Black Rook can, if BLACK desires, be moved onto h5 (ghost position) to capture this Pawn and remove it from the board.

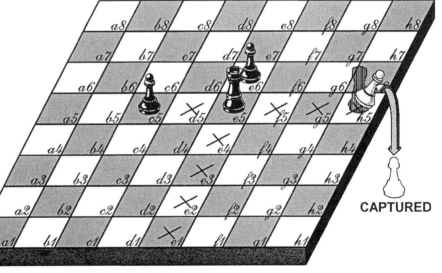

CAPTURED

The King Revisited

"Okay," drawled Gary Grouper, "we now know how a Rook can capture. But how about a King? Can he, too, capture enemy chessmen?"

"Oh, yes," said Sammy. "If an enemy chessman is on any of the squares to which a King can legally move, he, too, can move onto the square to capture that chessman" (Fig. 13).

Stella Starfish looked puzzled. "Do you *have* to capture an enemy chessman whenever it becomes possible?"

"Not at all," replied Sammy. "A player can choose *not* to move onto an enemy-occupied square and *not* to make a capture, if he or she doesn't want to."

Figure 13. By moving onto c3 or e4, the White King can capture a Black Pawn.

The Bishop

"What is this chessman with a slot cut into the top?" asked Joan Crawfish, holding it up in her claw.

Sammy placed it on the chessboard and said, "It's a Bishop. It is not so powerful as a Rook, but it does have a long reach. A Bishop can move as far as desired along the diagonals of a chessboard." So saying, Sammy marked with an x each square to which the Bishop could move (Fig. 14).

Figure 14. The Bishop on d5 can move onto any of the 13 squares marked x.

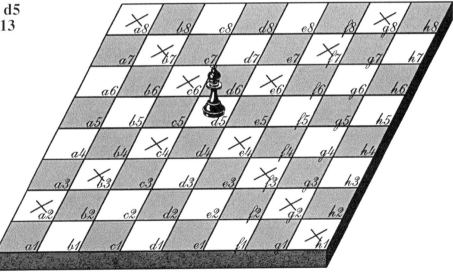

"What if its own chessmen are on some of the squares of a Bishop's diagonal?" asked Cary Grunt.

"Then the Bishop has to stop short, just as the Rook had to," answered Sammy (Fig. 15).

Stella Starfish then said, "I suppose that, if an enemy chessman occupies one of the squares of a Bishop's diagonal, the Bishop can capture it."

"Exactly," said Sammy. "To show you, I

Figure 15. The Bishop's own chessmen block it from moving the full length of its diagonals. Now it can move only onto those squares marked x.

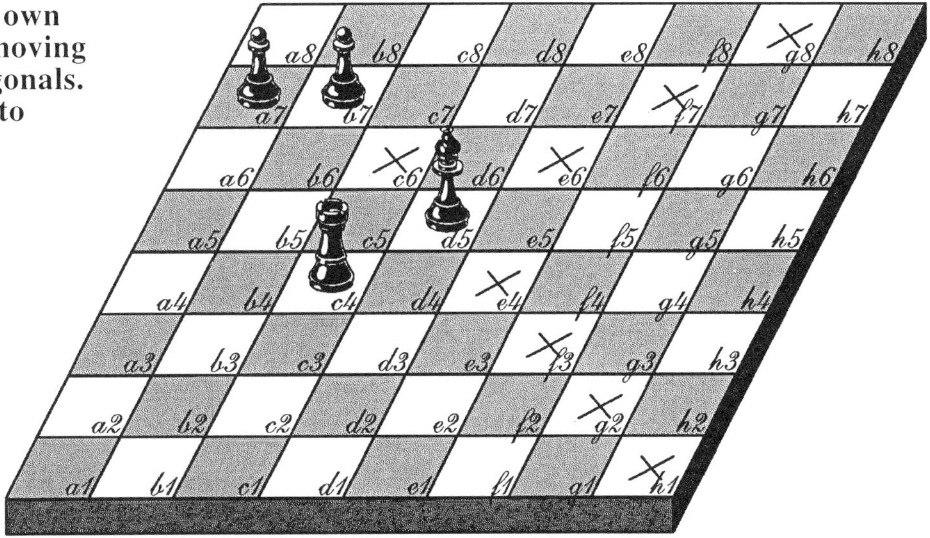

...l place a White Rook on square f3 (Fig. 16). This blocks the Black Bishop from moving onto squares g2 or h1. But he can move onto square f3 to capture the White Rook. If BLACK decides to make this capture, BLACK would remove the White Rook from the board (as shown by the curved arrow) and place the Black Bishop where the ghost image is on square f3."

Figure 16. The Black Bishop on d5 can move onto any of the squares marked *x*. It attacks the White Rook and can move onto f3 (ghost position) to capture this Rook.

CAPTURED

"BLACK's army includes two Bishops and so does WHITE's," Sammy continued. "The two Bishops for each army move along diagonals. But one moves along diagonals consisting of only black squares and the other moves only along diagonals consisting of white squares. Let me show you by putting WHITE's two Bishops (in their starting positions) on the board (Fig. 17). These two White Bishops are called **opposite-colored Bishops**. This does not refer to their own color but to the colors of the squares along which each must move."

Figure 17. WHITE's two opposite-colored Bishops in their starting positions. During a game, one will move only along black-square diagonals, the other only along white-square diagonals.

The Queen

"Now," said Sammy, "I'll bring out the most powerful of all the chesspieces, the Queen. Next to the King, she is the tallest of all the chessmen. She can move along ranks or files like a Rook, or along diagonals like a Bishop. What power she has! You can see this if I place the White Queen on the board and mark with an *x* each of the many squares to which she can move" (Fig. 18A).

"As for the Bishop and Rook, one of the Queen's own chessmen will block her from moving the full length of a rank, file, or

Figure 18A. The many squares to which a Queen on d4 can move. Note that she has the combined powers of a Bishop and a Rook.

diagonal. For example, because she is blocked by her own chessmen, the Black Queen can move only to the squares I have marked with x's" (Fig. 18B).

"What if an enemy chessman is on one of the squares to which a Queen can move?" asked Stella. "Can she move onto that square to capture it?"

"Yes, of course," answered Sammy.

"Do we now know how all the chessmen move?" asked Cary Grunt.

Figure 18B. The Queen's own chessmen (and the edges of the board) restrict her moves to the squares marked _x_.

The Knight

"Not quite," said Sammy. "I haven't talked about my favorite chessman, the Knight."

As he placed it on the board, Sammy exclaimed, "Isn't the Knight handsome? It is the only chessman that can leap over other chessmen. Its leap resembles an L, or an L as seen in a mirror. The leap covers two squares along a rank or a file, then one square at right angles to the two (Fig. 19). Note that **the square on which the Knight lands is**

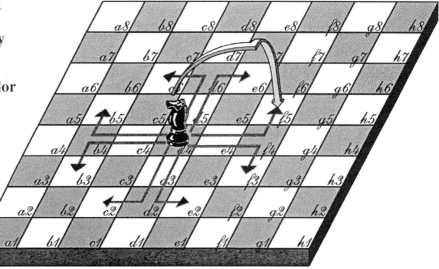

Figure 19. The Knight on d4 can leap onto e6, f5, f3, e2, c2, b3, b5 or c6 as shown by the shadows of his L-shaped leap. He always lands on a square that is opposite in color from his starting square.

always opposite in color from the square on which it started. The German word for knight, *Springer*, describes precisely how the Knight moves. It just springs off the square it is on."

Sammy continued, "I have now told you the way that most chess books describe the Knight's move, but I prefer a different way. I think of the Knight as starting from the bull's eye center of a square target, then leaping to a square of opposite color in the second 'ring' of the square target (Fig. 20). He can leap over other

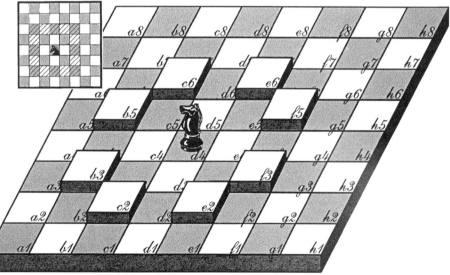

Figure 20. Imagine the Knight on d4 to be on the bull's eye of a square target (bird's eye view, upper left). He can leap onto any square in the target's second ring (ruled) if the square is opposite in color to the bull's-eye square. In the three-dimensional view these squares are upraised.

chessmen to land on these squares (Fig. 21). And he can capture any enemy chessman located on these squares—for example, the White Knight could capture the Black Pawn on e4, the Pawn on b5, or the Rook on a4.

"Super!" said Cary. "We now know all the moves. Let's play."

ASSIGNING VALUES TO CHESSMEN

"Not so fast," laughed Sammy. "There's more you need to know. For instance, during a chess game you try to capture the enemy chessmen and especially the King. Sometimes you can capture an enemy chessman without losing any of yours. But often you can capture an

Figure 21. What chessmen can the Black Knight capture?

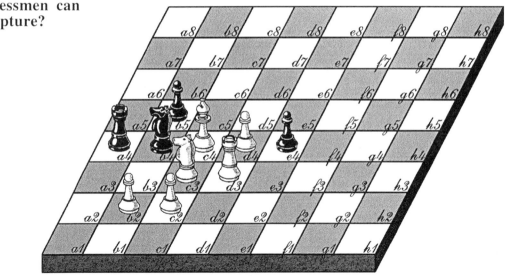

30

enemy chessman only by allowing the enemy, in turn, to capture one of yours. If so, it is called a **trade**. But you don't want to trade a Cadillac for a bicycle. So the big question is, 'What are the values of the various chessmen?' To show you, I'll mound up the sand next to each chessman according to how many Pawns it is worth. A Pawn is worth, of course, exactly one Pawn. But **a Knight or a Bishop is worth three Pawns; a Rook is worth five;** and **a Queen is worth nine**." To emphasize this, Sammy heaped up the sand into a three-Pawn-tall hill, a five-Pawn-tall one, and a nine-Pawn-tall hill (Fig. 22).

Figure 22. The number of Pawns each Piece is worth.

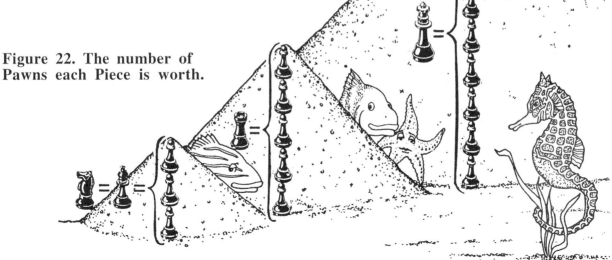

31

You would never want to trade a Queen for a Rook, unless it permitted you to capture the enemy King to win the game. But a trade of a Queen (= 9 Pawns) for a Rook (5 Pawns), a Bishop (3 Pawns), and a Pawn would be an even trade."

SETTING UP THE BOARD

"*Now* are we ready to play?" asked the ever impatient Cary.

"Not quite," said Sammy, "I need to teach you much more. But let's set up the board as if we're ready to play. When a game starts, WHITE's eight Pawns fill the entire second rank and BLACK's fill the seventh rank. The rest of WHITE's army fills the first rank and BLACK's fills the eighth rank (Fig. 23). Each Rook occupies a corner square, and each Knight is next to a Rook. That makes sense because, in the old days, knights often lived in castles and the Rook resembles the turret of a castle. Next to each Knight is a Bishop. I have now placed all the chessmen on the board except the King and Queen. As you can see, they will occupy the two center squares of each rank. But you can't plop them onto these center squares any old way. They have to be placed on precisely the correct center square. The rule is '**Queen to her color**.' In other words, I have to place them on the board (Fig. 23) so that the White Queen occupies the white square (d1) and the Black Queen rests on the black square (d8). The Kings occupy the remaining squares, e1 for the White King and e8 for the Black King. If you remember 'Queen to her color,' you will not make any mistakes when setting the King and Queen on the board. And the Bishops should be next to the Royal Couple. Check this, too."

Figure 23. When setting the board, the rule is "Queen to her color." This means that the White Queen should be placed on d1 and the Black Queen on d8. The Kings take what is left.

PAWNS, THE SOUL OF CHESS

"The great French chess master, Francois-André Philidor (1726-95)," said Sammy, "proclaimed Pawns to be 'the soul of chess.' In other words, how you play your Pawns often will determine whether you will win or lose. There's a lot you need to know about Pawns, for example, how they capture."

How Pawns Capture

"I know, I know," bubbled Stella Starfish, "a Pawn just moves forward in its file and bumps the enemy chessman off of it."

Sammy held back a smile and said, "No, that is not the way. The Pawn is the only chessman that captures by a move that differs from its ordinary move."

"How is that going to work?" asked Gary Grouper.

Sammy replied, "A Pawn can capture an enemy chessman only if it occupies a square diagonally in front of it. For example, as I have now set the board (Fig. 24), the Black Pawn on square b6 can capture a White chessman only if it is on either a5 or c5. So, you see, if it is BLACK's move, the Black Pawn can move onto a5 or onto c5 to capture a White Pawn. Similarly, the White Pawn on f4 can capture the Black Rook or Knight, but not the Black Bishop. And either of the White Pawns on a5 and c5 can capture the Black Pawn on b6, if it is WHITE's turn to move."

Chess was likely invented in northwest India between 500 and 600 A.D. An early reference (written in Sanskrit around 590-610) called the game "chaturanga." Then, as now, the Foot-soldiers (Pawns) could capture any enemy chessman located on a square diagonally in front of them. But they could move forward only one square at a time. Their two-square opening-move possibility is a later European invention.

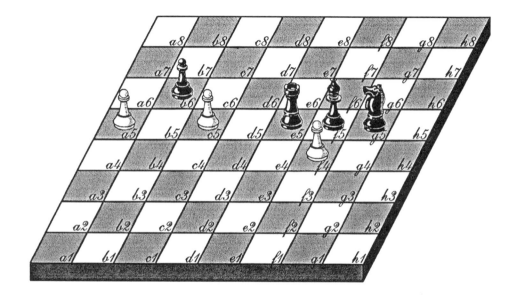

Figure 24. At its turn to move, a Pawn can capture any enemy chessman occupying a square diagonally in front of it. For example, if it is WHITE's move, a White Pawn can advance from a5 to b6 (or from c5 to b6) to capture the Black Pawn. Similarly, the White Pawn on f4 can advance to e5 to capture the Rook (or to g5 to capture the Knight). If BLACK has the move, the Black Pawn on b6 can advance to a5 (or to c5) to capture a White Pawn.

Blockaded Pawns

Sammy now continued, "If an enemy chessman occupies the square in front of a Pawn, the Pawn cannot move forward and is said to be 'blockaded.' As the board is now set (Fig. 25), the White Knight blockades the Black Pawn on f7, and the Pawns on g3 and g4 blockade each other."

"May we start playing now?" asked Joan rather politely.

En Passant Captures

Sammy answered, "Well, there's another tricky point you need to know. It's a rather unusual way by which a Pawn may, if the Player desires, capture an enemy Pawn. Suppose I have a White Pawn on g5 and you, Joan, have a Black Pawn on h7 (Fig. 26). And suppose you do not want me to capture it. How would you move it?"

Figure 25

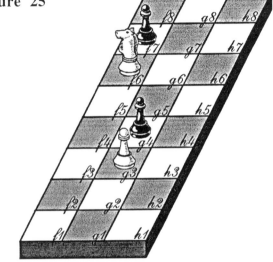

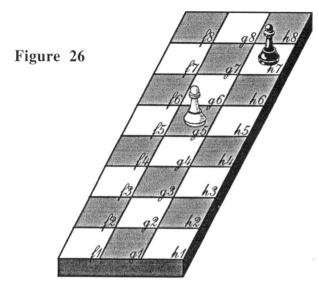

Figure 26

Joan studied the board and said, almost to herself, "If I move the Black Pawn from h7 to h6, the White Pawn will capture it." Then her face lit up as she said, "Aha, the Black Pawn on h7 has never been moved, so I'll move it *two* squares forward from h7 to h5 (Fig. 27A). Now the White Pawn won't be able to capture it."

Sammy smiled and said, "Good thinking, Joan. It is true that the Black Pawn, because it has not been moved before, can move two squares forward to h5. But there is a rule in chess that, if a Pawn moves two squares forward in order to escape capture by an enemy Pawn, this enemy Pawn can act on it as if it had only moved one square forward. Thus, the White Pawn can act as if the Black Pawn had only moved *one* square forward (to its ghost position on h6 in Fig. 27A). *If desired*, the White Pawn

Figure 27A

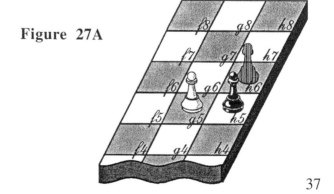

37

can move to the skipped square and capture the Black Pawn. This capture is called an *en passant* capture, *en passant* being French for 'in passing.' Here, I'll show you." And with this, Sammy moved the White Pawn as shown by the arrow and, using his tail, removed Joan's Black Pawn from square h5 (Fig. 27B).

Cary Grunt then said, "Sammy, I've got a question about *en passant* captures. Suppose that after Joan moved the Black Pawn from h7 to h5, WHITE moved another chessman instead of using the White Pawn to make the *en passant* capture. Can WHITE make the *en passant* capture on a later move?"

"No," said Sammy. "The *en passant* capture can only be made immediately after the enemy Pawn makes the two-square move. It can't be made later. This is a very important point. You have to strike while the iron is hot. If you don't, the chance is gone."

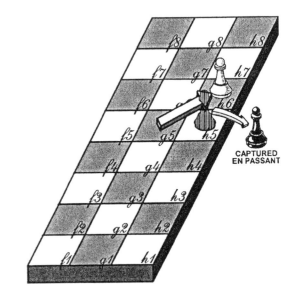

CAPTURED
EN PASSANT

Figure 27B. The White Pawn moves from g5 to h6 to capture, *en passant*, the Black Pawn that had moved from h7 to h5. This is the only capture in chess where the capturer does not move onto the square occupied by the chessman it captures.

RECORDING CHESS MOVES

"During informal games, chess players usually do not keep a record of their moves. But during tournaments, each Player records his or her moves as well as those of the opponent. When writing down moves," Sammy continued, "chess players use capital letters as abbreviations for the chessmen. These are as follows:

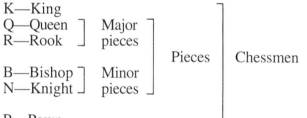

K—King
Q—Queen ⎤ Major
R—Rook ⎦ pieces

B—Bishop ⎤ Minor
N—Knight ⎦ pieces

P—Pawn

"Note the use of N for Knight because K is already in use to stand for King. Also note that **chesspieces** means *all* the chessmen except the Pawns. Because the Knight and Bishop have the least value of the pieces, they are called **minor pieces**. The Queen and Rook are called **major pieces**.

"When a Piece is moved, the Player writes down the capital letter that represents this piece, the name of the square from which it moved, then a short dash followed by the name of the square to which it moved. To illustrate, if a Bishop is moved from square f1 to b5, this move would be recorded as

Bf1-B5.

However, when a Pawn is moved, no one bothers to write the letter P, they just write the name of the square from which it moved, then a dash, and the name of the square to which it moved. For example, if a Pawn is moved from square e2 to e4, this move would be recorded as

e2-e4.

"I'll set up the board (Fig. 28) as if, for their first moves, WHITE advanced a Pawn from e2 to e4 and BLACK then advanced one from d7 to d6. As Figure 28 shows, WHITE's second move was to move a Bishop from f1 to b5. In writing down these moves, as I have already indicated, chess players use a short dash to stand for 'moves to.' And they would record these moves as

1. e2-e4   d7-d6
2. Bf1-b5

Notice that WHITE's moves are always listed in the left-hand column; BLACK's in the right-hand column." [**Editor's note:** Experienced players are even more brief. They would record these moves as

1. e4   d6
2. Bb5

As you can see, they omit the name of the square *from which* the chessman moves as well as the short dash. In other words they usually only write down the square to which the chessman moves.]

"Say," said Stella, "Bf1-b5 is a good move. The Black King is now in the White Bishop's line of fire."

"That's right," said Sammy, "and **whenever a chessman attacks the enemy King, the King is said to be 'in check.'** Years ago, whenever you made a checking move, you had to say 'check' to let your opponent know that his or her King was under attack. For beginners it is still a good idea to say 'check' when you attack the opposing King. But expert players are so aware of their King being under attack that, in tournaments, saying 'check' is mildly frowned upon because it may be distracting to your opponent. In recording your moves during a tournament, you would write the move we just made as

Bf1-b5+

where + stands for 'check.'"

Figure 28. The White Bishop moves from f1 to b5 to attack (check) the Black King.

41

"What can you do when your King is in check?" asked Joan.

"When your King is in check," Sammy answered, " you have to do one of three things: (1) move the King to a safe square; (2) capture the attacker; or (3) move one of your other chessmen into the line of fire so as to shield your King. If the attacker is a Knight, however, (3) will not work. He will leap over them. And now I want you to look at the board after the move Bf1-b5+, and tell me what BLACK should do to save the day."

After studying the board as drawn in Figure 29, Cary said thoughtfully, "The King has no safe square to move to, and there is no way that BLACK can capture the White Bishop."

He was interrupted by Joan who, clicking her claws with excitement, almost shouted, "Move the Pawn! Move the Black Pawn from c7 to c6." And so she made the blocking move (Fig. 30).

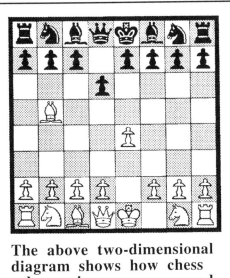

The above two-dimensional diagram shows how chess columns in newspapers and magazines would represent Figure 29 (facing page).

42

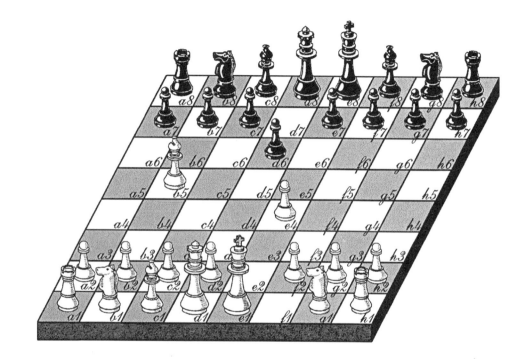

Figure 29. BLACK's King is under attack (check) by WHITE's Bishop. How can BLACK defend the King? Bc8-d7? Is there another good way?

"Excellent move," said Sammy, "and it would be recorded as c7-c6 because, as I mentioned before, players don't bother to write P when a Pawn makes a move." [**Editor's note:** As previously noted, experienced players would record the move as c6 because they do not usually name the square *from which* a chessman moves.]

"Wait a minute," said Stella, "if we move the Black Pawn onto c6, the White Bishop can capture it."

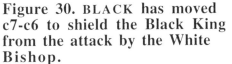

Figure 30. BLACK **has moved c7-c6 to shield the Black King from the attack by the White Bishop.**

PROTECTION

"True enough," said Sammy, "but then the Black Pawn on b7 could, in turn, capture the White Bishop. And who would want to trade a Bishop worth three Pawns for just a single Pawn?"

"So when the Black Pawn is on c6," continued Sammy, "it is said to be **protected or defended** by the Black Pawn on b7.

"Oh, yes, I see that now," said Stella. "In fact, my Knight on b8 could also capture the White Bishop if it moved onto c6 to capture the Black Pawn."

"Yes, indeed," replied Sammy, "the Black Pawn when on c6 is doubly protected. It is protected by the Pawn on b7 and by the Knight on b8. The White Bishop's check of the Black King has been removed because the Black Pawn, now on c6, shields the Black King. The White Bishop is now forced to retreat."

BEING EN PRISE

"Why must the White Bishop retreat?" asked Gary Grouper.

"Well, if this White Bishop is not moved, the Black Pawn will be able to capture it by the move c6xBb5. Note that an x stands for captures, and we read c6xBb5 as saying that the Pawn on c6 captures the Bishop on b5."

Sammy continued, "Whenever you have a chessman that will be captured if you don't move it, it is said to be *en prise*, which is French for 'in the grasp of.' In this case the White Bishop is in the grasp of the Black Pawn on c6. So the White Bishop is forced to retreat. Perhaps it moves Bb5-a4 (Fig. 31) so as to be no longer *en prise*."

After Sammy had moved Bb5-a4 to get the White Bishop out of danger (overleaf), his four students absolutely begged to start playing a real game. Joan was particularly keen to start and asked Sammy if they could.

"Well," replied Sammy, "you are not quite ready, but, if you like, I'll set up the board and be WHITE and the four of you can play as BLACK."

Figure 31. The White Bishop retreats (Bb5-a4) so as to be no longer attacked by the Black Pawn on c6.

QUEENS' SIDE AND KINGS' SIDE

Sammy continued, "Before we start, let me say one more thing. Chess players refer to the left half of the chessboard (as viewed by WHITE) as the Queens' side because, when a game begins, this half contains both Queens" (Fig. 32).

"How about the other half?" asked Gary. "Is it called the Kings' side because, when a game begins, it holds both Kings?"

"Precisely," said Sammy.

Figure 32.

BEGINNING A GAME

"Can we move first?" asked Stella.

"No," replied Sammy, you are playing BLACK and, in chess, WHITE always makes the first move to start a game. I have not told you this until now, but Pawns are named according to the file they occupy. So, when a game begins, each Player has an a-Pawn, a b-Pawn, a c-Pawn, and finally an h-Pawn. Often WHITE begins the game by moving her or his e-Pawn from e2 to e4 as I am doing now" (Fig. 33).

Figure 33. WHITE moves e2-e4 to open the game. This is an excellent opening that Bobby Fischer, the great American chess player, used with great success. It is the most popular opening move for WHITE.

"Why did you move the e-Pawn?" asked Gary. "Why not move the a-Pawn or the h-Pawn?"

Sammy replied, "In the beginning of a chess game, it is a very good idea to try to take control of the four squares at the very center of the board. It is almost like armies trying to capture a hilltop from which they can shoot down at the enemy. And, in chess, the four center squares d4, e4, d5 and e5 are like a tall hill (Fig. 34). Your chessmen, if in control of these four squares, are better able to swoop down and attack the enemy chessmen."

Joan then said, "Okay. I see why WHITE opens e2-e4. But now, how should BLACK move?"

Figure 34. The four crucial center squares. Try to control them.

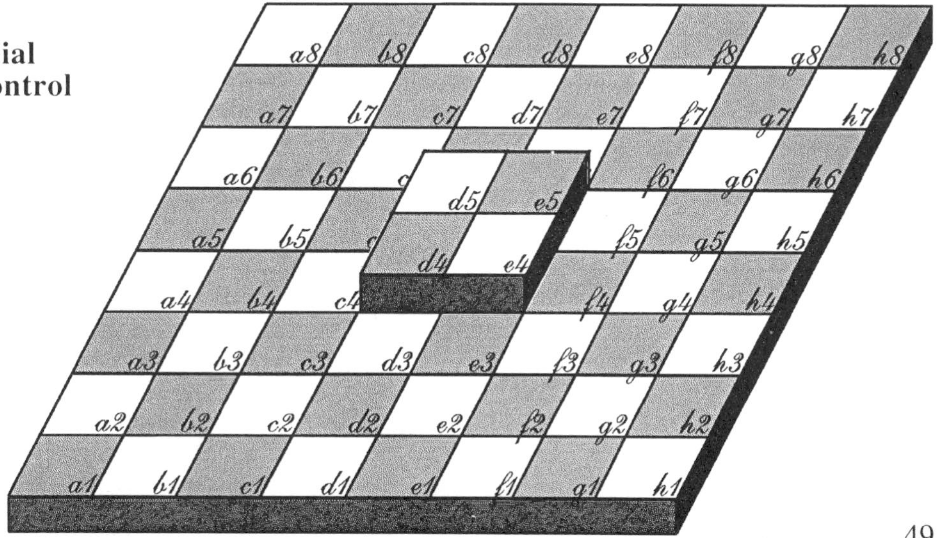

Sammy said, "Well, BLACK is not going to give up control of the four center squares without a struggle. So BLACK's move, called a reply to WHITE's move, often is to move the Black Pawn from e7 to e5. I'll make that move" (Fig. 35).

"During tournaments," said Sammy, "the moves are recorded and numbered in the order they were made. Thus, these first moves by WHITE and BLACK would be recorded as

1.   e2-e4   e7-e5.

Figure 35. The Black Pawn has moved from e7 to e5 in order to blockade the White Pawn on e4 (and to fight for control of squares d4 and f4).

Remember, WHITE's move is always written first and BLACK's second. But if you only want to mention BLACK's first move and not bother with WHITE's, you write it as 1. ...e7-e5. Here the three dots indicate that something is being omitted—in this case WHITE's first move."

"In reply to 1. ...e7-e5, WHITE's second move often is 2. Ng1-f3. So I will make that move (Fig. 36). Can you see why WHITE has made this move? In chess, whenever your opponent makes a move, you must always ask yourself, 'Why?'."

Figure 36. WHITE has moved 2. Ng1-f3. Why?

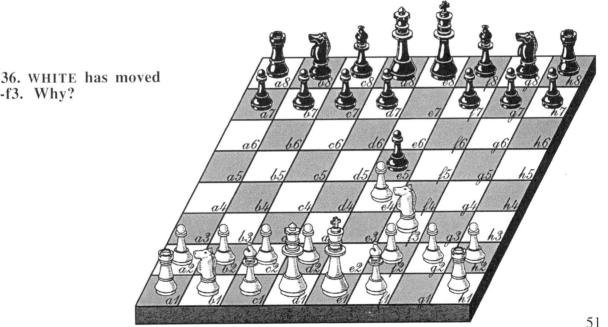

Cary and Gary swam in lazy circles above the board, studying it intently. Joan and Stella scuttled around the sides of the board to examine WHITE's last move. Soon, Gary said, "The White Knight, now placed on f3, attacks the Black Pawn on e5."

"Yes, indeed," said Sammy, "the brave White Knight has leaped into battle to attack the Black Pawn and to continue WHITE's fight to control the four center squares. So what should BLACK do?"

After a long pause, Stella said, "Joan, why not move the Black Knight from b8 to c6?" And so Joan, who also thought it was a good move, made the move 2. ...Nb8-c6 (Fig. 37).

"Great move!" said Sammy. "It does two things. The Black Knight now protects the Black Pawn on e5, but equally important, it also bears down on square d4 to continue BLACK's fight for control of the center."

THE SHORT NOTATION—As already noted (p. 40), experienced players use the short algebraic notation to record moves. This notation does not designate the square from which the chessman moves and also omits the symbol -, which means "moves to." The moves that produced Figure 37 would thus be recorded:

FULL		*SHORT*	
1. e2-e4	e7-e5	1. e4	e5
2. Ng1-f3	Nb8-c6	2. Nf3	Nc6

If two Rooks or two Knights can move to the same square, the short notation avoids confusion by adding a letter (or number) to indicate the file (or rank) from which the piece moved. Thus, in the example below, R2g3 and R4g3 indicate the two possible Rook moves to square g3. And Nfg1 and Nhg1 indicate the two possible Knight moves to g1.

Figure 37. The board after:

1. e2-e4   e7-e5
2. Ng1-f3   Nb8-c6

Sammy continued, "Now WHITE sometimes moves 3. Bf1-b5 (Fig. 38). This sequence of moves to open a chess game is called the **Ruy Lopez opening**; it is named after Ruy Lopez, a Spanish priest who in 1561 published a book on chess openings. Lopez favored this opening because it quickly gets WHITE's Knight and Bishop off WHITE's back rank (rank 1) and out where they can be more useful. Getting your chesspieces out where they can better attack the enemy and, at the same time, control the four center squares is called **development**. To this day the Ruy Lopez is a favorite opening for WHITE."

Gary then asked, "How does BLACK move after WHITE moves 3. Bf1-b5?"

Sammy had to think a bit because, after all, he had learned chess only by watching others play. Finally, after thinking about the different choices, he said, "Actually, BLACK has a choice of several moves. For his or her third

---

DEVELOPMENT—This is the race between WHITE and BLACK to move their pieces from Ranks 1 and 8 to squares nearer the board's center. There they become more effective and join the battle for control of center squares d4, e4, d5 and e5. As a rule of thumb, during development:

- Develop Knights before Bishops.
- Unleash your Kings'-side Bishop by advancing your e-Pawn.
- WHITE has the advantage of the first move and is thus a move (tempo) ahead of BLACK (who must play catch-up).
- Try not to move the same piece twice because squandering moves on a single piece may delay development of your other pieces.
- Don't bring your Queen out too soon. If you do, your opponent may gleefully develop pieces by moves that attack her. The result will be that you will be moving your Queen again and again while your opponent will be strongly developing his or her pieces.

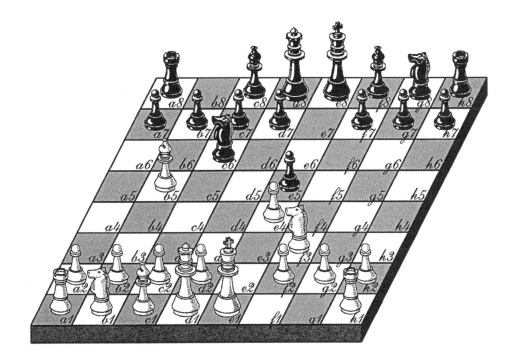

Figure 38. WHITE has just moved 3. Bf1-b5.

move BLACK often moves 3. ...a7-a6. Gary, why don't you make that move?" So Gary advanced BLACK's a-Pawn just one square (Fig. 39).

"The Black Pawn, now on a6, attacks the White Bishop."

"Oh, so it does," said Stella. "What can WHITE do about it?"

"WHITE has a choice of several replies," said Sammy. "One is to move 4. Bb5-a4 as I will

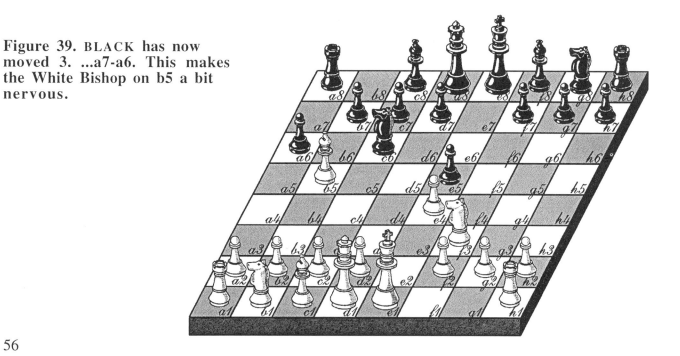

Figure 39. BLACK **has now moved 3. ...a7-a6. This makes the White Bishop on b5 a bit nervous.**

do now (Fig. 40). By retreating, the White Bishop escapes from the attack by the Black Pawn on a6."

"What is a good fourth move for BLACK?" asked Gary Grunt, his stripes shimmering in the light.

Figure 40. WHITE makes the move **4. Bb5-a4** so that the White Bishop is no longer under attack by the Black Pawn on a6.

"Often, BLACK moves 4. ...Ng8-f6," said Sammy as he made the move (Fig. 41). "Can you see the usefulness of this move?"

Cary Grunt and Gary Grouper swam in place above the board while Joan Crawfish and Stella Starfish crept around the edges.

Joan answered first. "By this move, BLACK develops his Kings' side Knight, moving him out from BLACK's back rank (rank 8) and, at the same time, attacking the White Pawn on e4."

Figure 41. BLACK has just moved 4. ...Ng8-f6.

58

CASTLING

"Excellent answer," said Sammy, "WHITE now quite often will use his or her fifth move to castle. **Castling is the only move in chess that permits you to move two pieces at the same time.** There are strict rules for castling. You can castle only if *the two pieces involved, the King and the Rook, have never*

been moved and *the squares between the King and Rook are unoccupied*. The correct way to castle is to (a) move your King two squares toward the Rook, and (b) leap-frog the Rook over the King (Fig. 42). *In castling, never move*

Figure 42. WHITE's fifth move is to castle on the Kings' side. The move is recorded as 5. 0-0.

59

the Rook first. If you do, it might be interpreted as just a move by the Rook. In Figure 42, WHITE castles on the Kings' side and records this fifth move as 5. 0-0, the symbol 0-0 indicating a Kings' side castling has taken place."

"What good is it to castle?" asked Stella.

"For one thing," Sammy replied, "it puts the King in a protective pocket that makes it more difficult for the enemy to attack him. For another, it unleashes a powerful piece, the Rook, so that it can join battle. This is one of the advantages to WHITE of the Ruy Lopez opening. It quickly develops WHITE's Bishop and Knight off squares f1 and g1 to permit a Kings' side castling."

"Can you only castle to the Kings' side of the board?" asked Gary Grouper.

"No," answered the Seahorse, "you can also castle on the Queens' side but at times it's less safe than castling on the Kings' side. To show you a Queens' side castle, I will reset the board as it might look after squares b1, c1, and d1 had been vacated (Fig. 43). To castle Queens' side, WHITE *first* moves the King two squares toward the Rook on a1, then leap-frogs this Rook over the King. As I said before, it would be a mistake to move the Rook first because your opponent might insist you were just moving the Rook and not allow you to castle. In recording moves, the symbol for a Queens' side castle is 0-0-0."

"So now we know all about castling," said Joan Crawfish.

"Not so," said Sammy," there are a few fine points. For example, if your King is in check, you cannot castle to get him out of check.

Symbols for Castling	
0-0	Castles Kings' side
0-0-0	Castles Queens' side

Figure 43. Example of a Queens'-side castling. WHITE moves the King from e1 to c1 and then leap-frogs the Rook from a1 to d1. A Queens'-side castling is recorded as 0-0-0. In this case it would be written as 0-0-0+ because it also places the Black King in check.

You also cannot castle if, when moving two squares toward the Rook, the King moves across a square that is under enemy control. For example, in Figure 44 WHITE cannot castle Kings' side because the Black Queen controls square f1. And a Queens'-side castle would not be legal because a Black Bishop controls square d1. In each case, the King, when castling, crosses over a square (marked *x*) that is under enemy control."

Figure 44. WHITE **cannot castle Kings' side or Queens' side because in castling the White King would be moving across a square (marked *x*) that is under enemy control.**

"Just to test you," said Sammy, "I will set up the board (Fig. 45) and ask: Can WHITE castle Queens' side?"

"No," replied Cary, "it is always illegal to move your King into check, and a Queens'-side castle puts the White King into check by the Black Bishop. That's as illegal as was moving a King through check when castling (Fig. 44)."

"How about if your King is checked? Can you castle to get out of check?" asked Cary.

"No, Cary, as I said before, that's illegal. You must get out of check some other way."

"Now I see," said Cary, "it is **illegal to castle into, through, or out of check**."

Figure 45. This Queens'-side castle would put the King and Rook in their ghost positions. Is it a legal move?

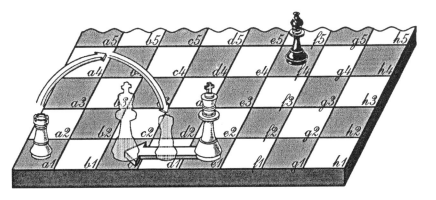

63

SAMMY DEFINES MATERIAL

"That sums it up, Cary," said Sammy. "And now I think that you are all ready to learn some of the ways to attack and capture enemy chessmen. If you can capture an enemy chessman without loss of your own, or if you can trade a lower-valued piece for a higher-valued enemy piece, you are said to gain an advantage in material."

"What do you mean by material?" Stella asked.

"Well, as you may recall," continued Sammy, "a Queen is worth nine Pawns; a Rook five; and a Bishop or Knight is worth three. So you can total up the worth of those chessmen you have on the board and compare it to the worth of those your opponent still has on the board. Whoever has the highest total is 'ahead on material.' To illustrate, suppose that besides your King you still have on the board a Queen, a Rook, and two Pawns. Your material then has a value equivalent to 16 Pawns (= 9 + 5 + 2). If your opponent has only a Queen, a Bishop, and one Pawn left (besides the King), their total value equals 13 Pawns (= 9 + 3 + 1). Thus, you have an advantage in material, and the Player with an advantage in material usually wins."

"Are there exceptions to this?" asked Gary Grouper who, for a grouper, had a very inquiring mind.

SAMMY DEFINES POSITION AND GAMBITS

Sammy replied to Gary's question, "Oh, very much so. You may be well ahead in material but yet lose the game because you are behind in position. **Position** is having your chessmen located on squares where they can best attack the enemy. If your chessmen so block each other that they cannot attack, your position is said to be poor. In a chess game the battle for position begins at once when each player tries to control the four center squares. Sometimes, to gain a favorable position, a Player may even allow a chessman, usually a Pawn, to be captured. Such a gift to your opponent is called a **gambit**."

"Can we start a real game *now*?" asked Joan. "You've been talking too long."

"Sorry about that," said Sammy, "but, as I said, I still need to teach you how the various chessmen attack or capture enemy chessmen. We will start with my favorite chesspiece, the Knight."

For 1500 years the move by the Knight, which began as the Horse (in chaturanga), has remained unchanged. By contrast, the Queen's moves have changed much (and greatly increased her power).

FORKING ATTACKS BY KNIGHTS

"The Knight becomes dangerous whenever he can find two or more enemy chessmen located on squares that are the same in color as the one he is on. In such case, the Knight may be able to leap onto the bull's eye square that controls these squares and thus attack both enemy chessmen at the same time. Such a simultaneous attack on two or more enemy chessmen is called a **fork**. I think it will be easier to show you than to tell you what I mean. So I will set up the board to permit WHITE's Knights to launch forking attacks on BLACK's chessmen."

Joan Crawfish now waited impatiently while Sammy placed chessmen here and there on the board. Finally, after he had placed two White Knights on the board, he said, "Study the board (Fig. 46) and tell me the best forking attack that WHITE can make. Then tell me WHITE's next-best forking attack."

Sammy's audience of four studied the board intently (Fig. 46). Joan was the first to see the very best fork that could be made. Fairly bubbling with excitement, she said, "Make the move Nb5-d6+."

"Outstanding!" said Sammy. "This fork (Fig. 47) would win the game because BLACK absolutely has to move his or her King. After the Black King moves, say, ...Ke8-f8, to escape the White Knight's attack, the White Knight will

Figure 46. The White Knight can make a devastating fork. Do you see it?

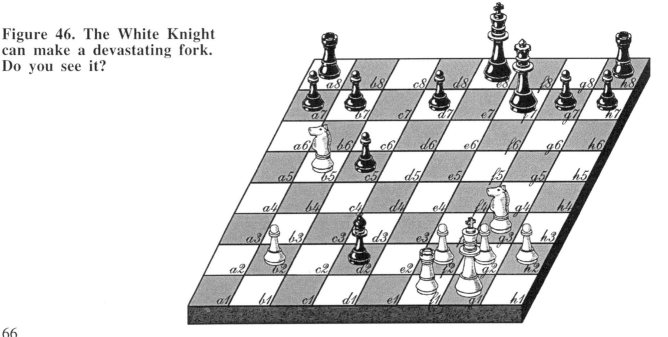

capture the Black Queen. Of course, the Black King will then capture the White Knight, but what a trade it is! BLACK has lost a Queen (worth nine points) and captured only a Knight (worth three points). Now BLACK is far behind in material. Sometimes, when a Player is so far behind in material that defeat seems inevitable, the Player lays the King on his side to indicate that he or she resigns, that is, admits defeat and gives up."

Figure 47. The White Knight pounces by moving Nb5-d6+ to fork BLACK's King and Queen. The Black Queen is history.

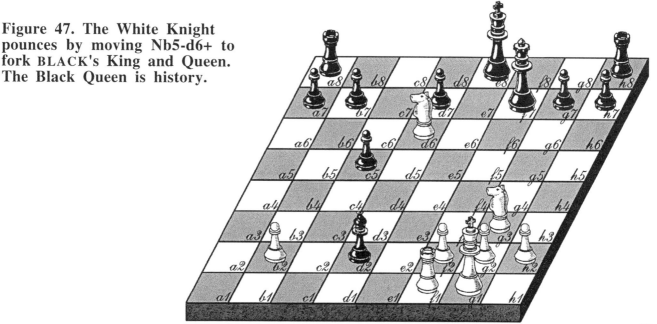

Sammy then said, "I will set the board as it was before Joan showed us that outstanding fork." Having done this (Fig. 48), Sammy asked them if they could see another fork. After a while Cary Grunt said, "Why not move Nb5-c7+? This also places the Black King in check so that, if BLACK can't capture the White Knight, BLACK has to move the Black King. After that, the White Knight will capture the Black Rook on a8."

Figure 48. Sammy returns the board to the way it was before Nb5-d6+ and asks if they can see another damaging fork by WHITE.

"Good move, Cary," said Sammy. "This fork of the King and Rook is a very common fork during games between beginning players. And as you say, when a Knight forks the enemy King and another chessman, unless the attacking Knight can be captured, the enemy King must be moved. And then the Knight captures the other chessman. Go ahead and make the move." So Cary made the move Nb5-c7+ (Fig. 49A).

Figure 49A. The White Knight has moved Nb5-c7+ to fork BLACK's King and Rook. Watch out for this fork.

Sammy then continued, "After the White Knight leaps onto square c7 to fork the Black King and Rook, BLACK makes the best of a bad situation by moving 1. ...Ke8-d8 (Fig. 49B).

Now, after WHITE moves 2. Nc7xa8 to capture the Black Rook (Fig. 49C), the White Knight is trapped. If he returns to c7, the Black King will capture him. If he moves to b6, the Black Pawn

Figure 49B. The Black King has moved 1. ...Ke8-d8 to prevent the White Knight from escaping after he captures the Black Rook on a8. Alternatively, 1. ...Ke8-e7 permits an even quicker capture of the White Knight after 2. Nc7xa8.

on a7 will capture him. The White Knight is a dead duck. In the moves to come, the Black King will move toward him, square by square, and thus capture him (Fig. 49D). But WHITE still comes out the winner by **winning the exchange**. This means that WHITE has captured a Rook but lost only a minor piece, in this case, a Knight.

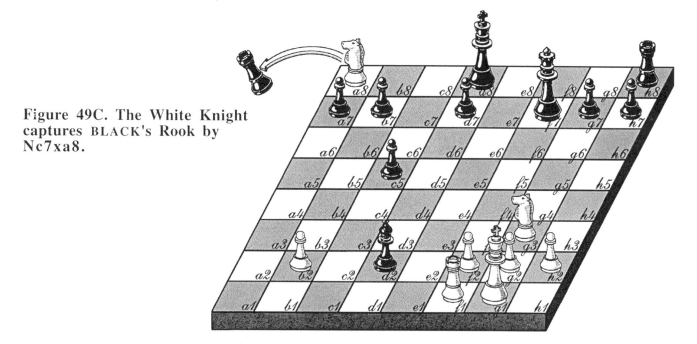

Figure 49C. The White Knight captures BLACK's Rook by Nc7xa8.

"Study the board (Fig. 49D) once more," suggested Sammy. "Do you see yet another forking attack?" The four students studied the board until Gary Grouper answered, "By moving Ng3-e4, the White Knight will fork BLACK's Bishop and Pawn."

"And now what should BLACK do? asked Sammy as he made the move (Fig. 50).

Figure 49D. After the White Knight moved Nc7xa8 to capture BLACK's Rook, BLACK moved ...Kd8-c8. The Black King will later move onto b8 to attack the White Knight and force its capture. But the damage is done. BLACK has lost a Rook and only won a Knight.

"How about ...Bd2-b4?" replied Stella.

"Ordinarily," answered Sammy, "that would be a good move because it is a common way to foil a fork. You **move one of the forked chessmen to protect the other**. Also, a Bishop on the square diagonally in front of its Pawn is a cozy arrangement. Each protects the other. In this case, however, it is a bad move because WHITE is a clever rascal and will move Ne4-d6+, to fork BLACK's King and Queen. Can the fork be foiled another way?"

Figure 50. WHITE moves Ng3-e4 to fork BLACK's Bishop and Pawn. Can BLACK avoid the loss of one or the other?

Cary answered, "Perhaps BLACK can move ...Qf7-d5."

"Excellent," said Sammy. "That's another way to foil a fork. **Move a chessman so that it protects both of the forked chessmen.**

Also, the move ...Qf7-d5 prevents the devastating fork Ne4-d6+ and, at the same time, the Black Queen attacks the troublesome White Knight on e4. As you can see, **good moves in chess usually serve several purposes.**"

Figure 51. BLACK **foils the fork by moving ...Qf7-d5. BLACK's Pawn and Bishop are now each protected by their Queen.**

"I am now convinced," said Stella, "that a Knight can be a pretty tough customer."

Not without pride, Sammy replied, "Yes, indeed, he is nimble and able to dart in and out among the other chessmen."

"Does the Knight have any weaknesses?" asked Joan.

WEAKNESS OF THE KNIGHT

"I am sorry to say he does," Sammy replied. "To show you, I will mark with an *x* every other square on the diagonals extending outward from the square occupied by a Knight (Fig. 52). It actually takes the Knight *four moves* to attack any chessman located on these *x*-marked

Figure 52. Only on its fourth move from d5 will the Knight be able to attack any chessman located on the squares marked *x*.

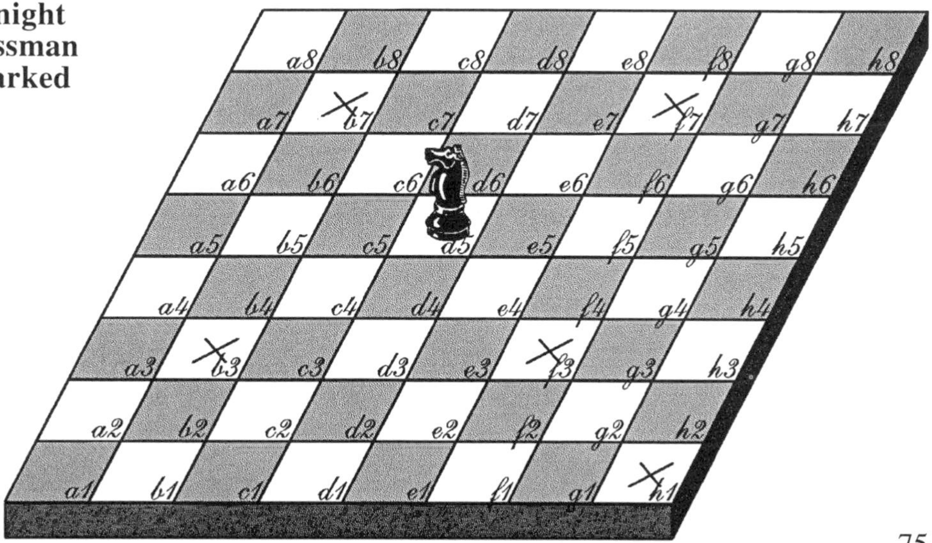

squares. I heard a worker say that in the book *Chess at a Glance*, Bloss called these squares 'Knight refuge' squares because, if you place a chessman on one, a pesky enemy Knight can't attack it until it moves four times. Try it."

SKEWERING ATTACKS BY BISHOPS

"If you have a Bishop running along black-square diagonals and if your opponent has two chessmen located on a black-square diagonal, you may be able to move your Bishop onto this diagonal to skewer them. A **skewer** is having two enemy chessmen both in the Bishop's line of fire. If the enemy chessman nearer to the Bishop moves aside, the farther one remains for the Bishop to capture. To illustrate skewers, I will again set up the board and ask you how WHITE's Bishop should move to

The Black Bishop has moved onto d1 to skewer the two White Rooks.

skewer enemy chessmen" (Fig. 53).

Dutifully, Joan Crawfish, Stella Starfish, Cary Grunt, and Gary Grouper studied the board. Cary and Gary swam in slow circles above it while doing so. Then Stella said, "The White Bishop on e2 has a choice of two skewering attacks."

"How so?" asked Sammy.

Figure 53. By what moves can the White Bishop skewer enemy chessmen?

"WHITE can move Be2-f3 to skewer BLACK's Knight and Rook." Stella continued, "But I also see a much better skewer, Be2-c4+!" (see the ghost positions in Fig. 54.)

"I am glad you said that last skewer with an exclamation point," said Sammy. "In chess books, whenever they describe an especially good move they put an exclamation point behind it. And, if it is a fantastically good move, they will even put *two* exclamation points behind it.

Figure 54. The White Bishop can move Be2-f3 to skewer BLACK's Knight and Rook, or it can move Be2-c4+! to skewer BLACK's King and Queen.

On the other hand, for bad moves they put a question mark behind them or, if especially bad, two question marks."

"That second skewer, Be2-c4+, is certainly a marvelous move," continued Sammy. "WHITE finds BLACK's King and Queen on the same diagonal and skewers them with the White Bishop. The White Bishop checks the Black King and, after the King moves to safety, the Bishop can capture the Black Queen" (Fig. 55).

Figure 55. After WHITE moved Be2-c4+ to skewer BLACK's King and Queen, the Black King then moved ...Ke6-d7 to get out of check. And now WHITE will capture the Black Queen by Bc4xf7.

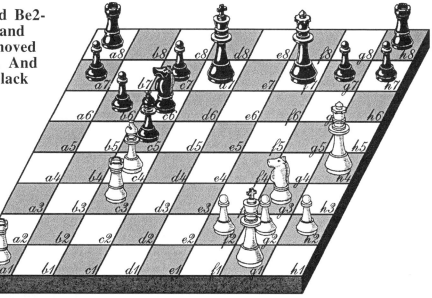

FORKING ATTACKS BY BISHOPS

If two enemy chessmen are positioned on the same diagonal, your Bishop can sometimes move onto this diagonal, but between them. The Bishop now attacks both chessmen at once, so this is a fork, not a skewer. Tell you what, I will set up the board so that WHITE can use a Bishop to make a forking attack. As soon as you recognize how, tell me the move." And so Sammy, using his tail, dragged the chessmen into new positions on the board (Fig. 56).

Figure 56. The White Bishop can fork two Black chessmen. Do you see the move?

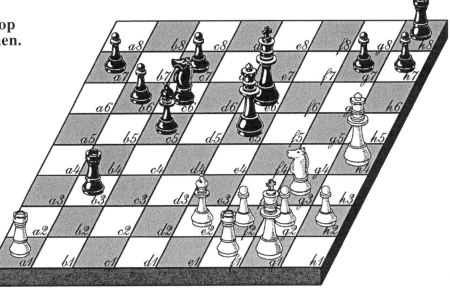

Almost at once, Cary Grunt said, "I see it! Just move Be2-c4+." And so he did (Fig. 57).

"Very good," said Sammy. "With this fork, the White Bishop attacks BLACK's Rook and King. Because BLACK *absolutely has to move or* *defend the King*, the White Bishop will capture the Black Rook by Bc4xb3."

"Does a Bishop have any weaknesses?" asked Stella Starfish as she crept around the edges of the board.

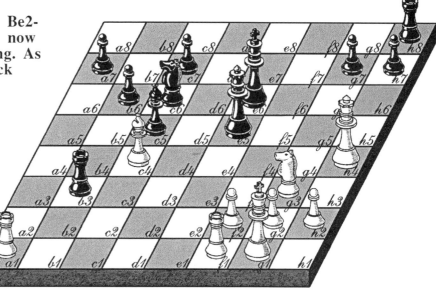

Figure 57. WHITE has moved Be2-c4+ so that the White Bishop now forks BLACK's Rook and King. As Sammy would say, "The Black Rook on b3 is history."

WEAKNESS OF THE BISHOP

"Yes, it does have a weakness that may set in near the end of a game, if you only have one Bishop left," replied Sammy. "When a game begins, each Player has two Bishops, one patrolling the black-square diagonals and the other the white ones. Then, if you lose a Bishop, say the one patrolling the white-square diagonals, your remaining Bishop, being confined to black squares, cannot attack any enemy chessman located on a white square. This puts a single Bishop at a disadvantage near the end of a game, especially if you do not have a Knight, a Rook or a Queen to attack chessmen on the squares that your Bishop cannot patrol."

"If your own Pawns mostly occupy squares of the same color as those patrolled by your Bishop, your Bishop may be so penned up behind them as to be unable to enter the battle. Such a Bishop is called a **Bad Bishop**. But it is truly not the Bishop's fault, it is the placement of your Pawns."

SKEWERS AND FORKING ATTACKS BY ROOKS

Sammy continued, "A Rook can also skewer and fork enemy chessmen, but it can do so only if they are located on the same file or rank. I will arrange the chessmen once again and, after I have, please study the board and tell me how WHITE should move to skewer Black chessmen."

Having said this, Sammy placed chessmen carefully on the board (Fig. 58). After he had finished, Cary and Gary swam above the board, studying it intensely. At the same time, Stella and Joan studied it from the side.

"I see *two* ways for the White Rook to make skewering attacks on Black chessmen," said Joan Crawfish, who seemed to have an excellent mind for chess. "Either Ra1-e1 or Ra1-

Figure 58. The White Rook can make two skewering attacks. What are they?

a3." And then she demonstrated both moves (Fig. 59).

"Very good," said Sammy, "but is one skewer better than the other?"

Sammy's four students studied the board intently (Fig. 59). Finally Gary Grouper said, "Neither will win a piece for WHITE."

"Why not?" asked Sammy.

Figure 59. The two possible skewers: Ra1-a3 or Ra1-e1.

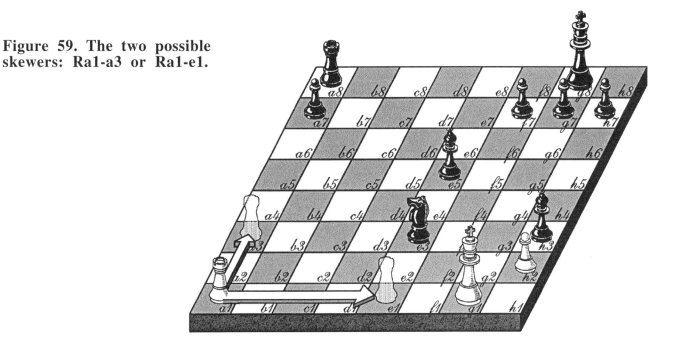

"Well," answered Gary, "if WHITE moves Ra1-e1, BLACK can move ...Be5-d4 (Fig. 60). Now the White Rook cannot capture the Black Knight because, if it did, the Black Bishop would, in turn, capture the White Rook. So 1. Ra1-e1 is a useless skewer. And 1. Ra1-a3 would be no better, because 1. ...Be5-d4 would foil it, too."

Figure 60. WHITE **moves Ra1-e1 to skewer** BLACK's **Knight and the Bishop on e5. But** BLACK **moves ...Be5-d4 to protect the Knight and foil the skewer.**

This same move, ...Be5-d4, would also foil the Ra1-a3 skewer by WHITE.

"There's a lesson to be learned here," said Sammy. "If your opponent skewers two of your pieces, try to protect the piece that is closer to the attacker. That often foils the skewer. And now that you are starting to think like chess players, let me show you that a Rook can fork as well as skewer."

"What's the difference? I am still not clear on that." Cary interrupted even before Sammy had finished setting up the board.

"If a chessman attacks two (or more) enemy chessmen *at the same time*, that is a fork," replied Sammy. "On the other hand, with a skewer your piece catches two enemy chessmen lined up on the same diagonal (if it is a Bishop), or on the same file or rank (if it is a Rook). It then moves onto this same line and directly attacks the nearer of the two enemy chessmen. Now, if this nearer chessman cannot be protected and has to be moved, your chesspiece has the farther of the two enemy chessmen *en prise* and can capture it. Look at the board as I have set it up (Fig. 61). By what move can a White Rook fork two enemy chessmen? And by what move can a White Rook skewer two of them?"

Joan, Stella, Cary and Gary studied the board intently. As usual, Cary and Gary swam slowly in circles above it so as to get a better look.

"I believe I see the fork," said Cary. "It is Ra5-b5."

"And I see the skewer," added Joan. "It is Rd1-b1."

To be sure that everyone understood the difference between a fork and a skewer, Sammy moved each Rook into the ghost positions shown in Figure 62A (page 88).

"Is there another fork?" Sammy asked.

"Hmm," said Stella, "the move Rd1-d4 will permit the White Rook to fork the two Black Knights. But I am not sure it is a good move."

Figure 61. Can you see the one skewer and two forks that a White Rook can make?

Figure 62A. The move Ra5-b5 (Rook moves to the ghost position on b5) forks two Black pieces—that is, attacks both at once. On the other hand, the move Rd1-b1 (Rook to the ghost position on b1) will skewer these same two Black pieces.

"Make the move anyway and tell me what is wrong with it." So the move was made (Fig. 62B). Each of the four students—Joan, Cary, Stella, and Gary—studied the board. Finally, Joan said, "Why, the Black Knight on square f4 can fork WHITE's Rook and King by moving

Figure 62B. By Rd1-d4, WHITE forks the two Black Knights. Why is it a bad move?

...Nf4-e2+! WHITE will lose a Rook."

Sammy said his favorite word, "Precisely," and then, with his tail, he made the move to show the others what Joan had already figured out (Fig. 63).

ATTACKS BY THE QUEEN

Sammy busily cleared the board of chessmen so that he could demonstrate the great power of the Queen in chess. He began by saying, "Remember, the Queen can move like a

Figure 63. After Rd1-d4, the Black Knight moves Nf4-e2+ to fork WHITE's Rook and King. Now, as Sammy always says, "The White Rook is history."

Bishop or like a Rook. This permits her to move great distances along ranks, files, or diagonals. And she can skewer and fork like a Rook or like a Bishop. Look at the board as I have set it up (Fig. 64) and tell me some of the attacking moves that the Queen can make."

Joan, who seemed to be learning the game rapidly, said, "The White Queen can move Qb1-a2 or Qb1-a1 to skewer the Black Bishop and Knight, that is obvious. Or she can fork them by moving Qb1-d3. Oh, yes, she can also fork the two Knights by moving Qb1-b6."

Figure 64. What attacking moves can the White Queen make to win some Black pieces?

"Good," said Sammy. "We will mark these moves with arrows (Fig. 65) but will not make them because there is one fork you missed."

After giving them time to study the board, Sammy asked, "Can you see the fork that Joan missed?"

Figure 65. The skewers (Qb1-a1 or Qb1-a2) and the two forks (Qb1-d3 and Qb1-b6) that Joan recognized. But she missed a very important fork. Do you see it?

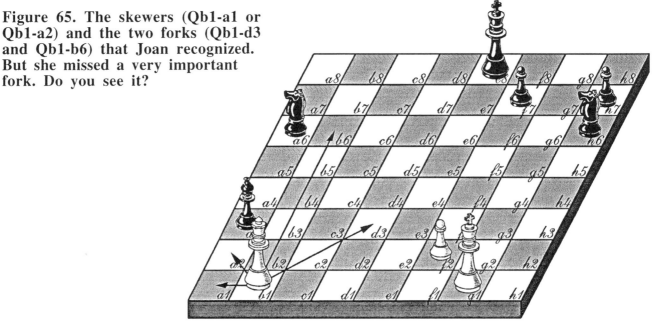

Stella answered excitedly, "Yes, I see it! The Queen can move Qb1-b5+. She now checks the Black King, and at the same time attacks the Black Knight on a6." So saying, Stella made the move Qb1-b5+ (Fig. 66).

"The beauty of it," Stella continued, "is that the Black King *has* to move out of check, and then the Black Knight on a6 becomes history. The White Queen captures him."

Figure 66. The fork Qb1-b5+ that Joan missed.

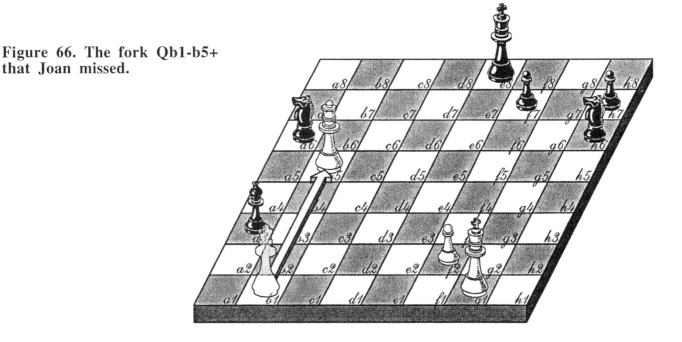

MORE ABOUT PAWNS

Queening a Pawn

Sammy said, "We have just seen the Queen, the most powerful chesspiece, in action. But now we will return to the Pawn, the chessman of lowest value. The Pawns are the foot soldiers of each Player's chess army. As Philidor said, they are the 'soul of chess' and how you handle them often decides whether you will win or lose. You will recall that Pawns move straight ahead in their file, one square at a time, except at their first move when, if desired, they can move two squares ahead. And, if your Pawn succeeds in passing through the enemy's army to reach the enemy's end of the board, a wonderful thing happens. The Pawn gets a battlefield promotion to become any chesspiece you want, except a King. Because a Queen is so powerful, a Pawn is almost always promoted to a Queen, and the process is called 'queening a Pawn.' If you choose a chesspiece other than a Queen, say a Rook, Bishop or Knight, this is called 'underpromoting.' Underpromoting rarely happens."

Gary now interrupted Sammy to ask, "How do you write down a Pawn promotion when recording your moves?"

"Good question," answered Sammy, "if a White Pawn moves from square g7 to g8 to become a Queen, you would write g7-g8 (= Q). For its underpromotion to a Knight you would write g7-g8 (= N)."

"Why would you ever ask for anything except a Queen?" inquired Joan, looking more puzzled than crawfish usually do.

"Another good question," replied Sammy. "Underpromotion is sometimes chosen if the new Queen, now located on the queening square, might stalemate the enemy King. If so, you might ask for a Rook provided it too did not stalemate the enemy King."

"What is a 'stalemate'?," asked Joan. This caused Sammy to squirm a bit because he realized that he had gotten ahead of himself. "That's right!" he said, "I have not told you what a stalemate is. And yet it is too soon to tell you now. I'll do it later." [*Editor's note:* He finally does so with Fig. 90 on page 132.]

"Say," said Gary, "what if you still have your original Queen and then you queen a Pawn? Where are you going to get a second Queen?"

Sammy laughed. "That's not a problem for most chess enthusiasts. Generally, they have a second set and can use a Queen from it. But if you don't, you can sometimes use an upside-down Rook to be the second Queen."

"But what if no Rook has been captured?"

"You've got me," chuckled Sammy. "I don't know what you can do. Maybe you can stick a label on the queened Pawn to indicate that it is now a Queen."

Having said that, Sammy went on, "As I have already said, games are often lost or won depending upon how a Player's Pawns are positioned on the board. So Pawn moves are very important. Many a game has been decided by Pawn promotions, Pawn captures, or Pawn forks."

Pawn Forks

"Pawn forks?" interrupted Cary. "Do you mean to tell me that a Pawn can fork enemy chesspieces?"

"Absolutely," replied Sammy, "as you

know, a fork is when you attack two opposing chessmen at the same time. And a Pawn is quite capable of doing this. To demonstrate, I will set up the board (Fig. 67) and ask you, 'What Pawn moves can WHITE make to fork Black chesspieces?"

Cary and Gary swam in slow circles above the board, and Joan and Stella scuttled around its edges. Then Cary said, "c2-c4 will fork BLACK's Rook and Knight."

"Good!" exclaimed Sammy, "that is a classic Pawn fork. Now when BLACK moves Rb5-a5 in order to save the Black Rook, the White Pawn will capture the Black Knight."

"Yes," said Stella, "but after the White Pawn captures the Black Knight, the Black Rook will capture the White Pawn."

"Quite so," said Sammy, "but WHITE has captured a Knight, which is worth three Pawns,

while losing only one Pawn. That gives WHITE an advantage in material." After a long pause, Sammy asked, "Can you see any other Pawn forks that WHITE can make?"

"How about e3-e4?" asked Gary.

"True, that move forks the Black Knight and Bishop, but the Bishop bites back and would simply capture the White Pawn by moving ...Bf5xe4. You would lose a Pawn by that move. Let's look at the board some more. Is there another Pawn fork?"

This time the four students studied the board long and hard. Finally, Joan said, "How about the move g2-g4?"

"Yes, yes," exclaimed Sammy. "The White Pawn, when moved onto g4, will fork BLACK's Bishop and Knight."

"Wait a minute," said Gary, "when I suggested the move e3-e4, you said that the

96

Black Bishop would bite back and capture the White Pawn. Won't this Bishop also be able to capture the White Pawn after it moves onto g4 to make the fork?"

"That's true," said Sammy, "but it is a different situation because when on g4 this White Pawn will be protected by the White Pawn on h3. So after the Black Bishop moves ...Bf5xg4 to capture the one White Pawn, then the one on h3 will capture the Black Bishop. So you will have lost a Pawn but won a Bishop. That's a good trade."

Figure 67. By what Pawn moves can WHITE fork Black chessmen?

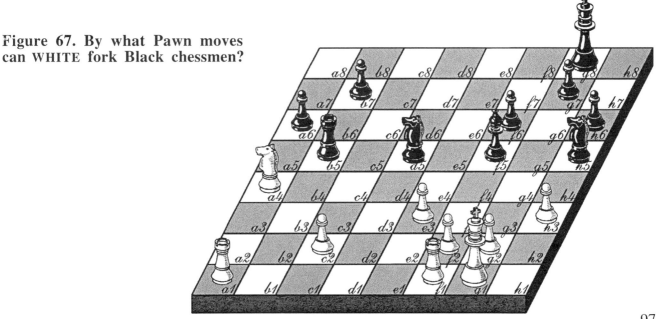

Sammy then drew arrows on the chessboard to demonstrate each Pawn fork that they had discussed (Fig. 68).

Passed Pawns

"I cannot emphasize too much that all Pawn moves must be made with great care," Sammy continued. "If you advance a Pawn to the wrong square, that error will not be correctable because Pawns can never move backwards."

"A Pawn can become extremely valuable and a constant worry to the other Player if it becomes a Passed Pawn." Cary then interrupted

Figure 68. The three possible Pawn forks by WHITE. However, e3-e4?? is a bad move.

Sammy to ask, "What's a Passed Pawn?" Sammy answered, "A **Passed Pawn** is one whose forward march to the queening square cannot be stopped by an enemy Pawn. I will set up the board to demonstrate this (Fig. 69). And now I will ask, 'Which of the three White Pawns is a Passed Pawn?'"

"Well," said Joan, talking almost to herself, "the White Pawn on a4 cannot move forward at all because it is blockaded by the Black Pawn on a5. And if the White Pawn on c5 advances to c6, the Black Pawn on d7 will capture it. Neither is thus a Passed Pawn. But the White Pawn on g6 is truly a Passed Pawn. There is no Black Pawn

Figure 69. How many Passed Pawns are on this board?

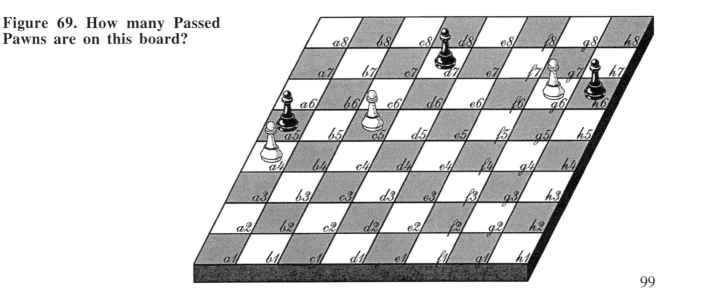

able to stop its march toward g8, its queening square. The h6 Pawn is also a Passed Pawn."

"Sometimes," continued Sammy, "a Player may have more Pawns on one side of the board then his opponent has. This is called a **Pawn majority**. If it occurs on the Queens' side, it is called a Queens' side majority. If on the Kings' side, it is called a Kings' side majority."

"What good is a Pawn majority?" asked Cary.

"Sometimes, Cary, a Pawn majority can be used to create a Passed Pawn to win the game. Let me set up an example." And so, once again, Sammy set up the board (Fig. 70A). He then continued, "As you can see, WHITE has a Kings' side majority while BLACK has a Queens' side

Figure 70A. Pawn majorities. WHITE has a Pawn majority on the Kings' side. On the Queens' side, BLACK has a Pawn majority.

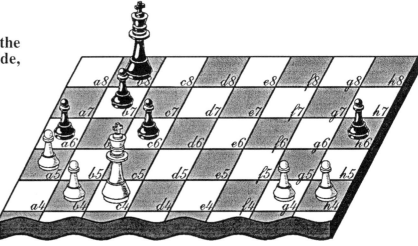

majority. If it is WHITE's move, WHITE can move 1. g4-g5 (Fig. 70B). After this move BLACK is doomed. It does not matter whether BLACK moves 1. ...h6-h5 or 1. ...h6xg5— WHITE will have created a Passed Pawn.

Figure 70B. WHITE moves g4-g5 and now, no matter how BLACK moves, WHITE will create a Passed Pawn.

Suppose BLACK moves 1. ...h6xg5 (Fig. 70C).
Then WHITE moves 2. h4xg5 to create a Passed
pawn (Fig. 70D). This White Pawn now has a
clear run toward its queening square, g8."

**Figure 70C. The board after
1. ...h6xg5.**

Figure 70D. The White Pawn has captured the Black Pawn by 2. h4xg5 and the Black King has immediately moved 2. ...Kb8-c8 in a desperate attempt to reach square g8 before the White Pawn. Who will win the race to g8?

Racing Toward the Queening Square

Joan Crawfish asked, "Can the Black King move toward square g8 in time to capture the White Pawn before it queens?"

"Good question," replied Sammy. "Unfortunately for BLACK the Black King will lose the race. He is too far away, by just one square, to catch WHITE's Passed Pawn."

"How do you know that so quickly?" asked Joan.

"There is a very neat way to figure it out," replied Sammy. "When only the two Kings and a few Pawns are on the board, and if a Passed Pawn exists, imagine a diagonal to be drawn from the Passed Pawn to the opponent's end of the board. This diagonal (dashed line Fig. 71) defines a large square whose sides consist of as many squares as are in the diagonal."

"I call this large square the **race square**, because that is the way I think of it. Now, if the enemy King is located within the race square—*or can move into it if it is his move*—the Passed Pawn is doomed to be caught before it can queen. As you look at the board (Fig. 71), and if you recall that it is WHITE's turn to move, you know that the Black King cannot win the race. It is not his move so he can't move ...Kc8-d8 or ...Kc8-d7 to enter the race square."

Gary asked, "What would have happened if it had been BLACK's turn to move?"

"Then," answered Sammy, "if BLACK has the move, the Black King moves immediately either ...Kc8-d8 or ...Kc8-d7. He is now in the race square and will reach f7 to capture the White Pawn the moment it reaches g8."

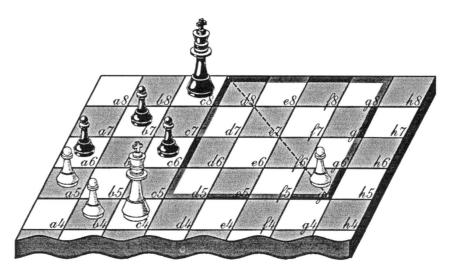

Figure 71. The Black King just moved 2. ...Kb8-c8 but, unfortunately for BLACK, he is still outside the race square (dark outlines). After WHITE moves 3. g5-g6, the squares g6, f7, and e8 will constitute the new diagonal and the race square will have shrunk to nine squares.

The race would go something like this (Fig. 72). After 5. g7-g8(=Q)+ the White Pawn turns into a powerful Queen that checks the Black King and stops him in his tracks. The hunted becomes the hunter.

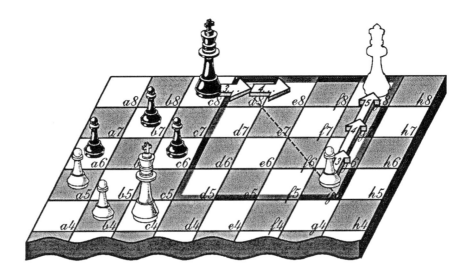

Figure 72. The Pawn on g5 wins the race to g8 as follows:
3. g5-g6 Kc8-d8; 4. g6-g7 Kd8-e8; 5. g7-g8(=Q)+.
If it had been BLACK's move, the Black King would have moved ...Kc8-d8 to enter the "race square" and capture WHITE's Pawn before it could queen.

Pawn Chains

"Players sometimes position their Pawns so that each is diagonally ahead of the other. Such an arrangement (Fig. 73) is called a **Pawn chain**. This is a strong Pawn formation because each Pawn in the chain protects the Pawn in front of it." Sammy continued his lecture, "The least advanced Pawn in a Pawn chain is called the chain's base. For example, the Pawn on c2 is the base of WHITE's Pawn chain and that on a7 is the base of BLACK's Pawn chain. The general rule is that if you want to break up your opponent's Pawn chain, attack its base."

Figure 73. Pawn chains.

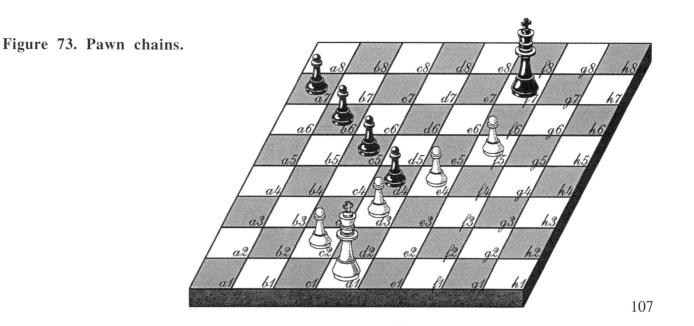

Doubled Pawns

Sometimes when a Pawn captures an enemy chessman, it ends up directly in front (or behind) a friendly fellow Pawn. The two Pawns are called **doubled Pawns** and are generally considered to be a weakness because, as I will show (Fig. 74), a single enemy pawn can blockade both of them. On the other hand, if the doubled Pawns occur near the center of the board, say in the *d* or *e* files, the arrangement may not be so bad. Indeed, if they help control the center squares they may even be quite useful. But a doubled Pawn in the *a* or *h* file is

Figure 74. WHITE's Pawns are poorly located.

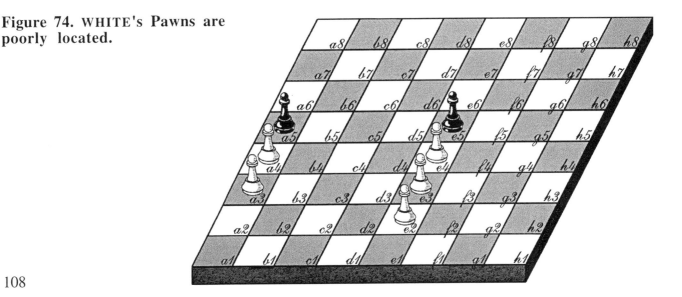

particularly bad.

"Sometimes," continued Sammy, "while trading equal-valued chessmen during a game, it may even be possible to cause your opponent to have tripled Pawns (Fig. 74). Tripled Pawns are really bad news. One enemy chessman can block all three and, even worse, tripled pawns are almost impossible to defend. One by one, they are bound to be captured.

THE POWER OF THE PIN

For three months, Sammy had now been teaching chess to his tank mates. And this morning he began their lesson by saying, "Sometimes, on the battlefield, a soldier or group of soldiers may be pinned down. In other words, the soldiers become trapped in a particular place, perhaps a building or a cave, and they cannot leave without exposing themselves to deadly gunfire by the enemy. In chess, too, you can sometimes pin down an enemy chesspiece so that it dare not leave the square it is on. If it should move off this square, it will expose an even more valuable enemy chesspiece, or the King, to the firepower of your Bishop, Rook, or Queen. These three pieces can pin down an enemy piece whenever they find that it and an even more valuable chesspiece are lined up on the same diagonal, file, or rank."

"It sounds to me like a skewer," said Joan. "As I recall, you taught us that, whenever two enemy chesspieces were located on the same diagonal, we could skewer them with our Bishop or Queen. Or if they were lined up on the same file or rank, we could skewer them with our Rook or Queen."

"Quite so," said Sammy, "but there is a difference. With a skewer you either win a piece or exchange a lesser-valued piece for a higher-valued enemy piece. With a pin, the nearer of the two pieces skewered is itself protected so you cannot capture it. But you prevent it from being moved off the square it is on. It is literally pinned to this square because, as I said, if it were moved, this would expose the more distant (and more valuable) piece to capture by the Bishop, Rook or Queen that you used to make the pin. And if the more distant piece is the King, it will be illegal to move the pinned piece because it would expose the King to check. A few examples should make this clear."   And with this, Sammy arranged the board to demonstrate some pins (Fig. 75).

"Can you see that there are five different moves that will pin pieces?" Sammy continued, "If it is WHITE's move, WHITE has a choice of four different moves that will pin Black chessmen. And if it is BLACK's move, BLACK can even pin a White chesspiece."

Cary and Gary swam in lazy circles above the board, studying it, and Joan scuttled around into WHITE's position while Stella occupied BLACK's. Soon Stella said, "If it is BLACK's move, how about 1. ...Ra8-a1?"

"Yes," said Sammy, "that pins the White Bishop on c1 against the White King. Now the Bishop cannot move off c1 because to do so would expose the White King to check. And, as I have said before, in chess it is an illegal move to expose your King to check—or to move your King into check. Study the board some more and tell me what pins WHITE can make if it is WHITE's move."

They all studied the board until Cary said, "If WHITE moves 1. Rg3-d3, the White Rook pins the Black Knight against the Black King."

Joan then broke in, "I agree, but I also see that the White Queen can make three moves, each of which will pin a Black chesspiece."

"Yes, you are right, Joan," said Sammy. "Who besides Joan can see what these three moves are?"

After a pause, Cary spoke up. "WHITE can move: 1. Qf4-g5 to pin the Black Rook against the Black King; or WHITE can move 1. Qf4-e5 to pin the Black Rook against the Black Queen; or WHITE can move 1. Qf4-d4 to pin the Black Knight against the King *and* the Black Rook

Figure 75. Can you see at least five moves that will pin pieces?

111

against the Queen."

"Wow!" said Gary Grouper. "The move Qf4-d4 is a double pin!"

"Precisely," said Sammy, who liked to say that word, "it is a very strong move because it does pin *two* of BLACK's chesspieces. And for review, let's mark all five pinning moves on the illustration" (Fig. 76).

"Let's assume," Sammy said, "that WHITE moves 1. Qf4-d4 to make the double pin. Can you see what WHITE's next move might be if BLACK does not guard against it?"

Gary spoke up, "Could it be the move c4-c5? The White Pawn attacks the pinned Black Knight. And because the Black Knight cannot move, the White Pawn will capture it."

"Very good," replied Sammy. "This is a frequent tactic in chess, that is, attack a pinned chesspiece with a Pawn in order to capture it."

Joan now said, "Before we go on, isn't there a skewer that we are overlooking? Why not move 1. Bc1-b2?"

Sammy smiled like the Cheshire cat and said, "I wondered when you would see that skewer. That could be the best move of all. It will allow you to trade the Bishop for the Black Rook on f6."

DISCOVERED ATTACKS

"There are times," Sammy said, "when one of your own chesspieces stands between an enemy chessman and one of your long-range pieces such as your Bishop, Rook or Queen. Now, when you move that in-between piece, the enemy chessman will be attacked by your long-range chesspiece. Such an attack is called a **discovered attack**. I will set up the board so that WHITE can make discovered attacks on some

Figure 76. The five pinning moves. Thus, ...Ra8-a1 pins the White Bishop against the White King. And Rg3-d3 or Qf4-d4 pins the Black Knight against the Black King. Qf4-d4 is a double pin because it also pins the Black Rook against the Black Queen. And finally, Qf4-g5 pins the Black Rook against the King. (*Editor's note:* A sixth pinning move, Qf4-d2, was overlooked by the fish.)

of BLACK's chessmen. I want you to study the set-up and tell me which is the best of all the discovered attacks possible." Sammy then used his tail to carry the chessmen around and set up the board (Fig. 77).

"How should WHITE move?" asked Sammy.

Gary Grouper flicked his tail in eagerness as, with some certainty, he said, "The move should be 1. Rf6-f8." And Gary made this move

Figure 77. The board is set for discovered attacks by both BLACK and WHITE. How should WHITE move?

(Fig. 78A).

"That is a marvelous move!" exclaimed Sammy. "If written in a chess book it would deserve to have an exclamation point behind it. Thus, 1. Rf6-f8!

"Actually," Sammy continued, "this discovered attack on the Black King by the White Bishop is called a **discovered check**. In fact, because the shielding chesspiece, the White Rook, now also checks the King, it is a **double check**." [Use ++ to record a double check.]

Figure 78A. WHITE moves Rf6-f8++ and the Rook checks BLACK's King. So does the White Bishop on h4. The two plus signs indicate this double check of BLACK's King.

115

"After WHITE moved 1. Rf6-f8++, why couldn't the Black Queen capture the White Rook?" Cary asked.

"She cannot do that because the White Bishop on h4 also has the Black King in check," Sammy replied. "That is the beauty of a double check. Your opponent cannot capture both attackers with a single move and thus has no option except to move the King. BLACK's only move is 1. ...Kd8-d7" (Fig. 78B).

Figure 78B. BLACK's King has moved ...Kd8-d7 to escape the check by WHITE's Rook and Bishop.

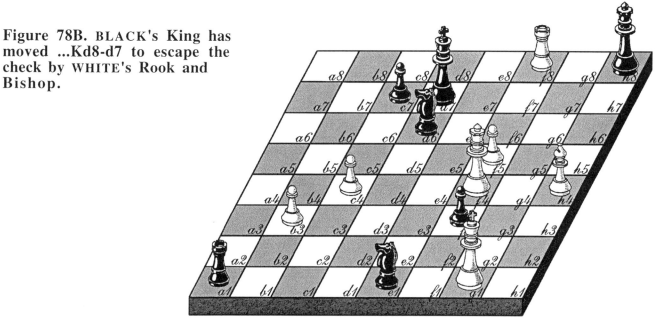

"And, now," Gary said triumphantly, "WHITE moves Rf8xh8 to capture BLACK's Queen" (Fig. 79).

"Yes, often that is the goal of a discovered check," Sammy replied. "You whisk away the piece that has shielded the enemy King from an attack by one of your long-range pieces (Bishop, Rook, or Queen). At the same time, you try to move this shield to where it attacks a valuable enemy piece. When the enemy King is moved, as it has to be, you then capture the valuable enemy piece with the former shield."

Sammy continued, "WHITE (p. 115) could also have captured the Black Queen by moving

Figure 79. After BLACK moved ...Kd8-d7, WHITE captured the Black Queen on h8 by Rf8xh8.

It is now BLACK's move. Can BLACK capture WHITE's Queen?

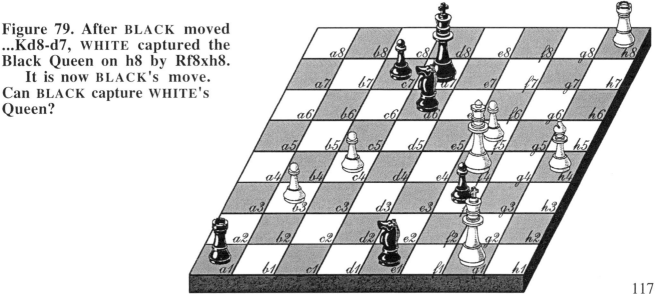

the shielding White Rook to h6 instead of f8, but then only the White Bishop would be checking the Black King. However, Rf6-f8++ is better because it results in a double check, and there is nothing more devilish than a double check.

"Now I will ask you another question. After losing the Black Queen, should BLACK tip over the Black King and resign?"

"No, I don't think so," said Stella. "After Rf8xh8, BLACK, too, can launch a discovered check on WHITE's King and with it capture the White Queen to even things up."

Figure 80. After the White Rook captured BLACK's Queen, BLACK counterattacked with a stunning discovered check, Ne1-d3+. WHITE's Queen, too, is history.

"Oh, I see it, too, Stella!" exclaimed Joan. "BLACK can move 1. ...Ne1-d3+. This whisks away the Black Knight to a square where it attacks the White Queen. *And*, at the same time, it unleashes a discovered check of WHITE's King by the Black Rook on a1. WHITE *has* to move the King and now the Black Knight will capture WHITE's Queen." So Joan made the move (Fig. 80).

Sammy beamed, "Excellent. As I said, you are all starting to think like chess players."

SAMMY DEMONSTRATES SOME CHECKMATES

Gary said, "When our attendants played chess, I did not watch them as closely as you, Sammy, but I did hear them say 'checkmate' and 'mate.' What does that mean?"

"Yes, I heard them, too," said Sammy.

"They said that the word 'checkmate' is from the Persian words 'shāh māt,' which mean 'The King is dead.' You say **checkmate** or **mate** if you check the enemy King and he cannot escape capture. In this case, you win the game. A checkmate differs from an ordinary check because not only is the enemy King under a successful attack, but he has no legal moves to escape this check. The enemy King is dead."

"What do you mean 'no legal moves'?" asked Gary.

"Actually, we have already discussed that, but I will explain it again. It is illegal for a King to move into check, that is, to move onto any squares controlled by enemy chessmen. I think it will be easiest to demonstrate what a checkmate is by setting up the board to show you. Indeed, I will set up the board and ask you to tell me the moves that WHITE can make to checkmate

BLACK. This first one you should see easily."
And so Sammy set up the board (Fig. 81).

No sooner was the board set up when Joan said, "Ra1-a8+ will checkmate BLACK."

"Yes, I thought you would see that quickly," Sammy said. "The Black King is under check and, being trapped behind his own pawns, has no move to escape. This particular checkmate is called a **back-rank checkmate** because the King is trapped on his own back rank (rank 8 for BLACK but rank 1 for WHITE). Back-rank checkmates may occur in games between

Figure 81. By 1. Ra1-a8+, WHITE will end up with a back-rank checkmate of BLACK. BLACK *can* move Be5-b8 or Bh3-c8, but these blocking moves will be useless because the White Rook will capture each Bishop (and continue to check BLACK's King).

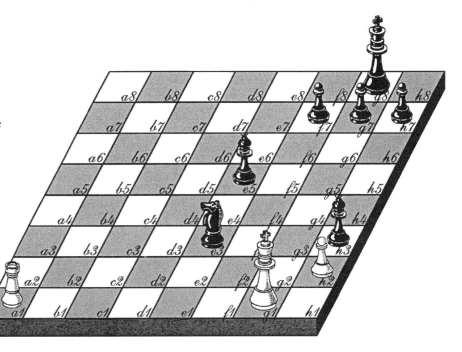

beginners but not in games between seasoned players."

Cary asked, "Could BLACK have prevented this?"

"Easily," said Sammy, "BLACK should have provided an escape hatch for the Black King by moving, say, ...h7-h6. If BLACK had done this earlier, then after WHITE moves Ra1-a8+, the Black King could escape by moving ...Kg8-h7.

"Let's discuss the gentle art of checkmating your opponent," Sammy continued. "What is the total number of squares to which a King can move if on a corner square? If on a square at the board's edge? If on a square nearer the board's center?"

Joan, who seemed to be a natural-born chess player, promptly said, "Three if on a corner square; five if at the board's edge; and eight if nearer the board's center."

BLACK provides an escape hatch for the King by ...h7-h6. If this had been done prior to Ra1-a8+ in Figure 81, the Black King could have escaped the back-rank checkmate by ...Kg8-h7.

Sammy said, "Precisely," and set up these three situations to show the others (Fig. 82). He continued, "As you can see, if on a corner square, a King has only three squares to escape to if checked. That is why, as we will see later, a lone King is often driven onto a corner square in order to checkmate him. On the other hand, it is more difficult to checkmate a King near the board's center because, if checked, he may have eight squares to escape to."

"Now I see why the back-rank checkmate worked," said Gary. "The Black King was at the

Figure 82. A King near the board's center has eight squares onto which he can move. At its edge he has five. If on a corner, he only has three.

122

board's edge and had only five squares to move to. And, unfortunately for him, three of these five squares were denied him because they were occupied by his own men. The White Rook simply moved onto the back rank and checked him while at the same time controlling the last two of his five escape squares."

"Now I will set up the board so that WHITE can once more mate in one (move)." So saying, Sammy used his prehensile tail to set the board as in Figure 83. "Can you see how WHITE can checkmate BLACK with just one move?" Sammy

Figure 83. WHITE to move and checkmate BLACK with just one move. Do you see it?

waited a long time, but none of his students answered. Finally, Sammy said, "WHITE's move is 1. Qa1-e5, checkmate.

"Note that, of the Black King's eight possible escape squares, c6 is occupied by his own Pawn and thus denied him. And the White Pawn controls c4. Also, the White Queen controls d4 and e5; the White Bishop controls d6 and, again e5; and the White Knight controls e4 and e6. As the board stands, the Black King has only one square to which he can legally move: c5. Now WHITE's Queen swoops onto e5 (Fig. 84) and,

Figure 84. The White Queen moves Qa1-e5+ to check BLACK's King. The Black King is checkmated because he has no squares to which he can legally move (every move would be into check).

because she is protected by the White Bishop, the Black King cannot capture her. In addition to checking the Black King, the White Queen also controls his last escape square: c5. He is checkmated because (1) he is under check by the White Queen *and* (2) any move he can make to escape will be illegal (because it will be a move into check by WHITE's Pawn or Queen).

"I have set up the board again (Fig. 85). And now we will assume that it is BLACK's turn to move. What is BLACK's next move?" asked Sammy.

Figure 85. What is BLACK's best move, if BLACK has the move. If WHITE has the move, do you see how WHITE can checkmate BLACK with just one move?

"That's easy," said Stella. "1. ...Qb4-e1 checkmates WHITE with a back-rank checkmate."

"Good," said Sammy, "but now let us assume that it was WHITE's turn to move (in Fig. 85) and not BLACK's. What should WHITE do?"

Cary said," Why not move h2-h3? This opens up an escape hatch so that the White King will not suffer a back-rank checkmate."

"Not a bad idea," said Sammy, "but there is a much better move for WHITE. With one move WHITE can checkmate BLACK. Do you see it?"

Gary Grouper stared goggle-eyed at the board while swimming lazily above it. After a long time of study he said, "Yes, I've got it. WHITE should move Rd6xf6. That checkmates BLACK."

"How so?" asked Cary Grunt. "If the White Rook captures the Black Pawn on f6, won't it in turn be captured by the Black Pawn on g7?"

"But the Black Pawn *can't* move off square f6, Cary. It is pinned there. Any move by it would be an illegal move, because the Black King would then be exposed to check by the White Queen. Here, let me show you." And to demonstrate this, Gary made the move Rd6xf6+ (Fig. 86). "Now you can see that g7xf6 is an illegal move."

"Congratulations, Gary," said Sammy, "you looked ahead a couple of moves and figured out the moves that would checkmate your opponent. In many chess games, however, neither player wins and the result is a *tie* or a **draw**."

DRAWS

Sammy continued, "In chess a game can end in a draw if each Player agrees that he or she cannot defeat the other. Usually, one will offer the other a draw and the other, if he or she agrees, will accept this draw."

"Is that the only way that a game can end in a draw?" asked Stella.

"Oh, no," replied Sammy, "a draw will also result if a Player, even if he or she is far behind in material, can cause the same position of the chessmen to be repeated three times in a row. Look at the board as I have just set it up (Fig.

Figure 86. With the board as set in Fig. 85, WHITE has moved Rd6xf6+! The Black King is checkmated. Note that ...g7xf6 is illegal because it exposes BLACK's King to check (by the White Queen).

87). WHITE is far behind in material but has the move. Can you see a move that WHITE can make to force the same position to be repeated three times and allow WHITE to escape with a draw?"

Joan said, "That is easy. WHITE should move

1. Rf1-a1+. This forces BLACK to move 1. ...Ka8-b8 (Fig. 88). But now WHITE moves 2. Ra1-b1+ to check BLACK's King and force the move 2. ...Kb8-a8. WHITE cannot capture BLACK's King but WHITE does have him trapped

Figure 87. WHITE to move and force a draw.

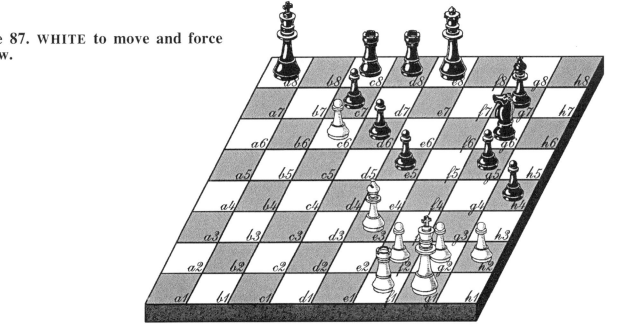

so he can only move back and forth between a8 and b8. And by moving the White Rook back and forth between a1 and b1, WHITE can force BLACK to move the Black King back and forth between a8 and b8 forever."

Sammy interrupted to say, "But three times is enough. WHITE needs only to announce that he or she will repeat the attacks to make the position repeat itself for a second and a third time. After the third repeat, the game is declared a draw.

Figure 88. WHITE **has moved 1. Rf1-a1+. This forced** BLACK **to move 1. ...Ka8-b8. Next,** WHITE **will move 2. Ra1-b1+ to force the Black King to move back onto a8.**

WHITE has slithered out from what appeared to be a certain loss.

"Even if you cannot cause the same position to repeat for three successive times, there is another way to force a draw." Sammy continued, "It is called a **perpetual check**. I have set up the board to show you an example (Fig. 89). Assume it is BLACK's move and, being far behind in material, BLACK will be delighted to achieve a draw. To do this, BLACK

Figure 89. BLACK to move and achieve a draw through a perpetual check.

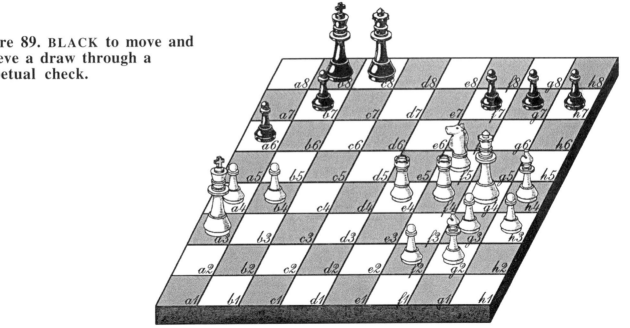

moves 1. ...Qc8-c3+. And when WHITE moves 2. Ka3-a2, BLACK moves 2. ...Qc3-c2+. After this WHITE can move either 3. Ka2-a3 or 3. Ka2-a1. In any case, the Black Queen can check the White King again and again and again. It's a perpetual check, and thus a draw results."

"Say," asked Stella, "let's go back to the example you gave us of a position repeated three times in a row (Fig. 88). Wasn't that a perpetual check?"

"Yes, it was," replied Sammy. Actually, the three-move-repeat draw generally involves a perpetual check. But in the last example (Fig. 89), because WHITE can move either 3. Ka2-a3 or 3. Ka2-a1 in response to 2. ...Qc3-c2+, WHITE can certainly delay, if not avoid, having the same position repeat three times. But there is no doubt that WHITE's King cannot escape check after check after check by the Black Queen. So it

is a perpetual check, and BLACK changes a lost game to a draw."

"Have we now discussed all the ways that a draw can occur?" asked Gary Grouper.

"No," replied Sammy, "there is still one more way, and it is called **stalemate**."

"Stalemate?" questioned Gary. "What a strange word."

"Actually," said Sammy, "it is a strange situation as well. It happens when the only chessman that a Player can move is the King *and the King is not in check*. Yet every move that this unchecked King can make is an illegal move (because it would move the King into check)."

"That sounds confusing," said Cary. "Can you set up the board to demonstrate a stalemate, please?"

So Sammy removed most of the chessmen that had been on the board and set it up again

(Fig. 90). "Look at the board," said Sammy. "If it is BLACK's turn to move, does BLACK have any legal moves?"

The four students studied the board (Fig. 90) and could see that the only chessman BLACK could move was the Black King. And yet, every move possible for BLACK was an illegal move into check.

"Note," said Sammy, "that if the Black King moves onto d8 or f8, he will be moving

Figure 90. It is BLACK's move, but BLACK has no legal moves. Any move by the Black King would be illegal (into check). A stalemate exists, and the game is a draw.

into a check by the White Pawn on e7. And if he moves onto d7 or f7, he will be moving into check by the White King. He has no legal moves to make *but he is not in check.* So it is a stalemate, and the game is a draw."

THE THREE PARTS OF A CHESS GAME

"Are we ready to begin playing a real game now?" asked Joan.

"Not quite. There is a bit more I need to teach you. For example, a chess game is usually considered to be divided into three parts: (1) the **Opening**, which consists of about the first ten or fifteen moves; (2) the **Middle Game** during which you try to achieve passed pawns and to fork, skewer, pin or make discovered attacks; and (3) the **Endgame** when relatively few chessmen remain on the board and your King

becomes a useful and active piece."

The Opening

"We have already discussed a good part of the Opening, and you may recall that it usually begins with a fight to control the center squares. At the same time, you try to develop your pieces, that is, bring them out from your back rank (= rank 1 for WHITE and rank 8 for BLACK). In developing them, you try to place them on squares from which they can attack any enemy chessmen located on the four center squares. As a general rule, it is better to develop Knights before Bishops. Once your Knight and Bishop no longer occupy squares f1 and g1, you will be able to castle on the Kings' side. And generally it is better to castle Kings' side than Queens' side. Don't wait too long to castle because it places your King in a protective pocket and, at the same time, gets your Rook off a corner square and into the battle.

"Another good idea is not to move the same piece twice during the first 10 or 15 moves. At times this cannot be avoided, but you will be in trouble if you move the same piece over and over while your opponent is steadily developing *several* pieces toward the board's center (where they will be thorns in your side). Also, don't bring your Queen out too soon. If you do, your opponent will attack her with Bishops, Knights or Rooks. She will then be moving again and again and again while your opponent is, at the same time, developing these attacking pieces.

"And that brings us to an important point. Good moves in chess often serve more than one purpose. Sometimes you can develop a piece and, at the same time, attack an enemy piece. If your opponent now has to defend or move the pieces you attack, you gain a move in developing your pieces. Equally important, your opponent may waste a move. As I said before, if you bring your Queen out too early, such bad things may happen to you."

"So," interrupted Gary, "you should never bring your Queen out during the Opening game?"

"Never is a strong word," answered Sammy. "On rare occasions a Queen *may* be brought out early to your advantage. But *usually* this is not so."

The Middle Game

"We are not going to talk much about the Middle Game, because it is best learned by actual play," said Sammy. "Besides, the Middle Game includes all the methods of attack—the forks, skewers, and pins—that we discussed earlier."

"Good," said Joan, "I for one am ready to

play."

But Cary asked, "How do you know when the Middle Game begins?"

Sammy replied, "No one can pinpoint when the Opening ends and the Middle Game begins because the Opening blends gradually into the Middle Game. And the Middle Game, just as gradually, blends into the Endgame."

The Endgame

Sammy continued, "During the Endgame most of the pieces, and especially the Queens, will no longer be on the board. Now his majesty the King can safely step out and himself become a powerful attacking piece. He stalks enemy Pawns that are not protected either by other Pawns or by their King. Many a game is won or lost during the Endgame. Or a lost game can be turned into a draw. As a result, entire books have been written about the Endgame. But I know you all want to start playing actual games, so I will just teach you a few of the principles and possibilities related to the Endgame."

SOME PRINCIPLES OF THE ENDGAME

The Opposition

"During the endgame, the King that has the opposition often has a great advantage."

Stella interrupted Sammy by asking, "What do you mean, 'has the opposition'?"

"That is easier to demonstrate than describe," replied Sammy. "Suppose the two Kings are on the same file and are separated by one square (Fig. 91). The King who has moved last is said 'to have the opposition.' As a result, he can prevent the other King from moving forward. For example, suppose that in Figure

91, WHITE has just moved and thus 'has the opposition.' The Black King cannot dodge past the White King if WHITE does not want him to. The moves might be 1. ...Kc6-d6, 2. Kc4-d4, 2. ...Kd6-e6, 3. Kd4-e4, and so on (Fig. 91). The White King, because he has the opposition, can continually block the Black King from moving forward into WHITE's territory."

"Besides that, what is so good about having the opposition?" asked Cary.

Figure 91. The White King has just moved and thus has the opposition. As a result, he can prevent the Black King from moving forward (toward the reader).

"Well, I will set up the board and show you a case where WHITE will win if he or she has the opposition but must settle for a draw if BLACK has the opposition. For the board as I have now set it (Fig. 92), we will assume that WHITE has the opposition and, therefore, that it is BLACK's move. How should BLACK move?"

In response to Sammy's question, his four students carefully studied the board. And then Stella said, "BLACK should move 1. ...Kf8-e8."

Figure 92. It is the Black King's turn to move, and thus WHITE's King has the opposition.

"Precisely," said Sammy, "when trying to prevent a Pawn from queening, the opposing King's best tactic is to move in front of it so as to control the enemy Pawn's queening square, in this case e8 (Fig. 93). That is BLACK's correct move, but will it prevent the White Pawn from queening?"

Gary answered, "No, WHITE will move 2. e6-e7 to advance the White Pawn and force BLACK to move 2. ...Ke8-d7. This allows WHITE to move 3. Kf6-f7 and gain control of the queening square. Now, BLACK cannot prevent the White Pawn from queening" (Fig. 93).

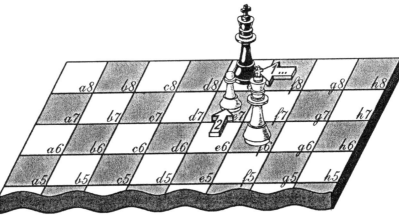

Figure 93. BLACK moves 1. ...Kf8-e8 and WHITE moves 2. e6-e7. BLACK's next (and only) move, 2. ...Ke8-d7, allows WHITE to move 3. Kf6-f7. Once on square f7, the White King controls e8, the queening square. As a result, the White Pawn is now sure to queen.

"Very good," said Sammy, "but let's go back to the original position (Fig. 94A), except that now BLACK has the opposition. WHITE thus has to move and can only advance the Pawn by moving 1. e6-e7+. The Black King then moves onto the queening square by 1. ...Kf8-e8. After these moves (Fig. 94B), WHITE loses all hope of queening the Pawn. Why?"

Figure 94A. This is precisely the same set-up as in Figure 92 except that the Black King has the opposition (and thus it is WHITE's turn to move).

The four students once more studied the board intently. After a long pause, Gary said, "The White King has to stay on a square touching square e7 in order to defend the White Pawn. If he does not, the Black King will capture the White Pawn. I think that the White King must move 2. Kf6-e6."

"Yes. And after 2. Kf6-e6 the board will look like this" (Fig. 95), said Sammy. "Now it is BLACK's move once more, but where should BLACK move?"

Cary Grunt answered, "The Black King cannot move onto d8 or f8, because either would be a move into check by the White Pawn. And he

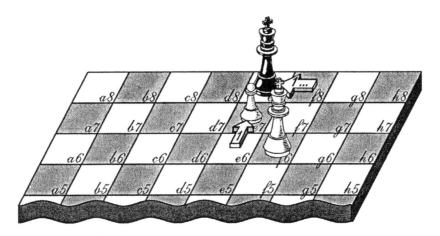

Figure 94B. After 1. e6-e7+, BLACK moves 1. ...Kf8-e8, and now WHITE *must* move 2. Kf6-e6. Any other move will lose the Pawn.

140

cannot move onto squares d7 or f7 because each would be a move into a check from the White King."

"It looks like the Black King (Fig. 95) has no legal moves," said Stella, "but yet he is not himself in check."

"And what does that mean when a King, who is not in check, has no legal moves (and has no friendly chessmen that can be legally moved)?" asked Sammy.

"Why, that means that the Black King is stalemated!" exclaimed Joan.

"Precisely," said Sammy, "and a stalemate means a draw. BLACK has gained a draw even though WHITE has a Pawn only one square from its queening square. Now do you see how

Figure 95. The board after WHITE moved 2. Kf6-e6. It is now BLACK's move, but BLACK has no legal moves. Wherever the Black King moves, it will be into check. It is a stalemate.

important it was to have the opposition?"

The students were impressed. They could see that, with the board set as it had been in Figure 92 or 94A, WHITE could queen the White Pawn and thus win only if, at that point, he or she had the opposition. Otherwise, BLACK could force a stalemate and achieve a draw.

Creating a Passed Pawn

Sammy continued, "Not only do Kings become attacking pieces during the Endgame, but Pawns increase greatly in value, especially if they are Passed Pawns. Put on your thinking caps now because I am going to set up the board so that three White Pawns, which have advanced into BLACK's half of the board, are opposed by three Black Pawns."

So saying, Sammy arranged the board as in Figure 96A. Sammy then asked, "Suppose it is WHITE's turn to move. How should WHITE move to create a Passed Pawn to win the game?"

This was indeed a hard question for Sammy's students to answer. None could. So after waiting a long time, Sammy said, "WHITE should push the middle Pawn forward by moving 1. c5-c6." So he made the move (Fig. 96B).

The other fish cried, "You're giving away a Pawn!" Cary was so disturbed he rubbed his teeth together to make the grunting sounds for which grunts are famous.

Sammy laughed at their dismay. "It's not as bad as it looks. Actually, by pushing this middle Pawn, WHITE will win the game."

"It's true," he continued, "that BLACK will capture this Pawn. Indeed, BLACK absolutely *has* to capture this Pawn either by b7xc6 or by d7xc6. It does not matter which so let's say BLACK moves b7xc6." He then made this

Figure 96A. WHITE to move and create a Passed Pawn that will be able to queen.

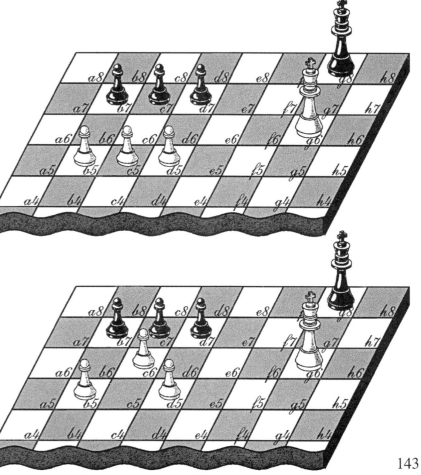

Figure 96B. WHITE pushes the middle Pawn forward (c5-c6)!

143

move, too (Fig. 97). "But now," Sammy said,
"WHITE wins with d5-d6" (Fig. 98).

**Figure 97. After b7xc6, BLACK
has doubled pawns on the c-file.**

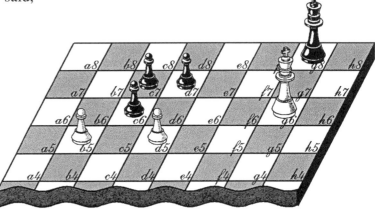

**Figure 98. WHITE moves d5-d6 so
that each of BLACK's doubled pawns
is now under attack by a White Pawn.
Only one of the attacking White
Pawns can be captured. The other
will be able to queen.**

Recommended Tactics

"During the Endgame are there things that you should do, and others that you should not do?" asked Stella.

"There are," said Sammy. "As a rule, if you are a Pawn ahead it is a good idea to exchange pieces, especially Queens, whenever an even trade can be made. For example, if you have besides your King—a Queen, a Rook, a Knight and a Pawn, you have material equal to 18 Pawns (9 + 5 + 3 + 1) to aid your King. And if your opponent has the same pieces but no Pawn, his or her material equals 17 Pawns (9 + 5 + 3). Now, a material advantage of 18 to 17 is not much. But if you succeed in exchanging Queen for Queen and Rook for Rook, then your Knight plus Pawn represents a strength of (3 + 1) or 4 and your opponent's single Knight represents a strength of 3. You now have a 4 to 3 advantage that is proportionally better than an 18 to 17 advantage. And if you can trade Knights, you will have a King plus Pawn versus a King."

STANDARD ENDINGS
King plus Pawn versus King

"Many chess games end up with a King and Pawn against a lone King," said Sammy. If you have the Pawn and your King can control the squares in front of it, especially its queening square, you will be able to queen the Pawn and win. If you can't, you will likely end up with a draw. On the other hand, if it is you who has the lone King, you try to prevent the enemy King from getting in front of his Pawn to run interference for it.

"If your Pawn is on one of the two end

files, file a or file h, then even if you do get your King in front of it, you will not be able to queen it if the enemy King can control the queening square (a8 or h8). You will find out that as long as the lone King stays near the queening square, a stalemate and thus a draw will result.

"As we have already seen," continued Sammy, "sometimes even a Pawn on files b to g can be prevented from queening if the enemy King has the opposition."

King and Rook versus King

"A fairly common ending," Sammy lectured, "is a King and Rook against a lone King. It is also a fairly easy win. The King and Rook try to herd the lone King toward a corner square in order to checkmate him. The lone King tries to avoid this, but if he can't, he tries to achieve a stalemate. Let's start with a lone Black King near the center of the board (Fig. 99), and see how WHITE uses his King and Rook to force the Black King toward the corner where he can be checkmated. The series of moves could well be as follows":

	WHITE	BLACK
1.	Kd3-e3	Kd5-d6
2.	Ke3-d4	Kd6-c6
3.	Re4-e5	Kc6-d6
4.	Kd4-e4	Kd6-d7
5.	Ke4-d5	Kd7-c7
6.	Re5-e6	Kc7-d7
7.	Kd5-e5	Kd7-c7
8.	Re6-d6	Kc7-b7
9.	Ke5-d5	Kb7-c7
10.	Kd5-c5	Kc7-c8
11.	Kc5-b6	Kc8-b8

Figure 99. Sammy advises the Reader to set up a board like this and then to make the moves listed on page 146 (to see how a King and Rook checkmate a lone King).

"I know you could not follow all those moves without having moved the chessmen on the board but, believe it or not, some chess masters can play **blindfold chess**. In blindfold chess they call out their moves without seeing the board. Somehow they keep in their heads the positions of all the chessmen after their moves and after their opponent has called out his or her move. Two players can actually play each other 'blindfold' while taking a walk. They do not need a board or chessmen.

"For example, after BLACK's last move 11. ...Kc8-b8, in their heads they will know that the board looks like this" (Fig. 100).

"As you look at the board, can you tell me what WHITE's best move is?" asked Sammy.

Gary said, rather promptly, "12. Rd6-d8 checkmate."

"Good," said Sammy, "notice how the White King prevents the Black King from moving onto rank 7 so that Rd6-d8 checkmates him."

King and Queen versus King

"A King and Queen against a lone King is an even easier win than King and Rook against a lone King. It is so easy," said Sammy, "that the Player with the lone King will usually resign. So we need not play it out."

King and Minor Piece versus King

"How easy is it for a King and a Knight or a King and a Bishop to checkmate a lone King?" asked Cary.

"Actually," Sammy said, "it is impossible. A King and a single Knight—or a King and a single Bishop—cannot checkmate a lone King and the game will be a draw. A King and a minor piece just can't do the job."

Figure 100. WHITE to move and checkmate BLACK.

King and Two Bishops versus King

"Can a King and two Bishops checkmate a lone King?" asked Stella.

"Yes," said Sammy, "that is a definite win. You bring the two Bishops so that they are side-by-side on two neighboring squares, just as I have done" (Fig. 101).

"I have marked with x's the squares controlled by the two Bishops so you can see that the Black King is now imprisoned behind two diagonal walls. At the same time the White King blocks any forward move of the Black King, forcing him to remain on the 8th rank. To emphasize this I have also marked with x's the three 7th rank squares controlled by the White King. So if it is WHITE's move, what is the first step toward herding the Black King toward the corner?" asked Sammy.

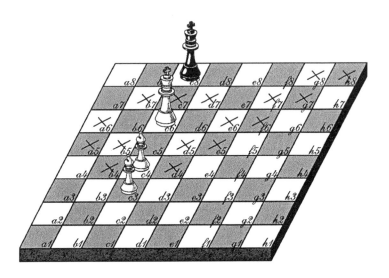

Figure 101. To checkmate a lone King, two Bishops occupy neighboring squares to form diagonal walls that trap the lone King in one corner of the board. At the same time, their King keeps the lone King penned up against the side of the board.

150

Cary and Gary swam in slow circles above the board while Joan and Stella crept around its sides. All studied it intently. Ultimately, Cary said, "The move should be 1. Bc3-f6. This prevents the Black King from moving away from the corner. Let me show you." So saying, Cary made the move (Fig. 102).

"Excellent," said Sammy, "and BLACK's only possible move is 1. ...Kc8-b8, which brings the Black King closer to the corner (Fig. 102). But, now, what should WHITE's next move be?"

Cary, who had evidently figured out the moves, said, "WHITE must now move 2. Kc6-b6. The White King thus retains the opposition and prevents the Black King from advancing onto the 7th rank. BLACK can now move 2. ...Kb8-c8 to stay away from the dreaded corner square, but then WHITE moves 3. Bc4-e6+ to

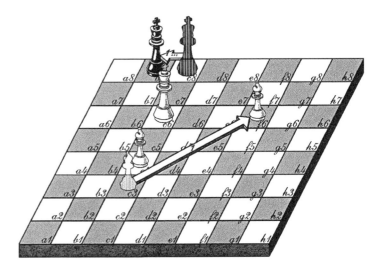

Figure 102. WHITE **moves 1. Bc3-f6. The Black King now has to move 1. ...Kc8-b8. How should** WHITE **move next?**

151

Figure 103A. WHITE has moved 2. Kc6-b6 and BLACK, fighting to stay away from the corner, has moved 2. ...Kb8-c8. WHITE now moves 3. Bc4-e6+. BLACK then has to move 3. ...Kc8-b8 (back to the ghost position) to escape check.

check the Black King. After these moves the board will look like this" (Fig. 103A).

"And now," Joan broke in, "the Black King is doomed. He has to move 3. ...Kc8-b8 and the two Bishops sweep him toward corner square a8

by (Fig. 103B):

4.   Bf6-e5+   Kb8-a8
5.   Be6-d5+   checkmate."

"Good job," said Sammy. "The Black King fought to stay away from the corner square

Figure 103B. The two Bishops force the Black King into a corner where, with help from their King, they can checkmate him.

153

where he knew he was doomed. But he was forced there, anyway."

"Wait a minute, let's back up a few moves." said Gary. "What if BLACK, instead of moving 2. ...Kb8-c8, had moved 2. ...Kb8-a8?"

"In that case, after that move, the board would look like this," said Sammy as he moved the chessmen to their positions in Figure 104. "And, I would ask myself 'Why was BLACK making it easy for me by moving the Black King

Figure 104. BLACK has moved 2. ...Kb8-a8. If WHITE moves Bf6-e5, what will be the result?

154

onto the corner square?' In chess it is always wise to ask yourself why your opponent moved the way he or she did. Do you see what BLACK is hoping for? There is one move we should not make."

Joan answered, "We certainly don't want to move 3. Bf6-e5. This would stalemate the Black King and we would have to settle for a draw."

"Precisely," said Sammy. "Always be on your guard when an opponent seems to be making it easy for you."

King, Bishop and Knight versus King

"A King, Bishop and Knight can checkmate a lone King, but it is not easy," said Sammy. If both Players are skillful, it will take over 30 moves to checkmate the lone King. With less skilled players, it may take many more. In fact, if you have the lone King, don't resign. Just try to stay as far away as possible from the corner squares that are the same color as the squares the enemy Bishop is patrolling. If this Bishop is operating on the light-colored squares, keep your King away from the light-colored corner squares. This brings to mind another way to get a draw that I have not as yet told you about."

"What rule is that?" asked Stella.

"It is the **50-move rule**," answered Sammy. "If both Players each make 50 successive moves without advancing a Pawn or capturing a chessman, the game can be declared a draw. Of course, you would only know this if all the moves of the game were being recorded."

King and Two Knights versus King

"A King and two Knights cannot checkmate a lone King unless the Player with the lone King makes some bad mistakes. By avoiding corner squares, the lone King can achieve a draw (through the 50-move rule). If cornered, he can achieve one by stalemate."

OUTCOMES AGAINST A LONE KING

Easy Wins
K + Q (or K + R)—They force the lone King to the board's edge.
K + 2B—The three force the lone King to a corner square.

Harder Win
K + B + N—The three force the lone King to a corner square controllable by the Bishop.

Draws
K + 2N—If lone King avoids corners.
K + N (or K + B)—A draw no matter what.

RAMBLING ROOKS
Rooks on Open Files

Gary Grouper began the usual morning chess lesson by asking, "What is an open file, Sammy?"

"An **open file** is a file that does not have any Pawns on it." And now Sammy said with great emphasis, "WHENEVER THERE IS AN OPEN FILE, MOVE YOUR ROOK ONTO IT." Having said this, Sammy arranged the board so that the d file was an open file (Fig. 105A). He then asked, "If it is WHITE's move, what move do you suggest?"

Joan Crawfish replied, "You practically shouted that we should locate Rooks on open files, so I think WHITE should move 1. Ra1-d1."

After she made the move (Fig. 105A), Sammy said, "Yes, of course. Now you can see that the White Rook is like a long-range cannon that can fire from one end of the board to the other. It can ramble up and down any open file and occupy any square not controlled by an enemy chessman. And, during games between inexperienced players, the Rook can sometimes move all the way down the file to execute the enemy King with a back-rank checkmate."

"After 1. Ra1-d1, what can BLACK do?" asked Cary Grunt.

"BLACK now has to fight WHITE for control of the open d file. To do so, BLACK might move

Figure 105A. The d file is an open file, and WHITE moves 1. Ra1-d1 to try to gain control of it.

1. ...Ra8-d8 to place one of his or her Rooks on it." Sammy himself made the move (Fig. 105B).

"Wait a minute," said Stella, "WHITE can now capture this Black Rook by 2. Rd1xd8."

"And that is exactly what WHITE will do," replied Sammy. "But BLACK does not care because either the Black Rook on f8 or the Black Bishop on g5 can, in turn, capture the White Rook. Likely, BLACK would make the capture with the Rook by moving 2. ...Rf8xd8. Now BLACK's Rook would control the open file."

Figure 105B. BLACK moves 1. ...Ra8-d8 to fight for control of the open file.

"Has WHITE now lost the battle for control of the open file?" Stella asked.

"No, not at all. WHITE can move 3. Rf1-d1 to continue the battle." And after these moves—2. Rd1xd8 Rf8xd8 followed by 3. Rf1-d1—the board looked like Figure 106.

As the board now looked, it worried Stella. "Isn't that a bad move?" she asked. "Can't the Black Rook move 3. ...Rd8xd1+ to capture the White Rook and cause a back-rank checkmate of WHITE's King?"

"No, the Knight on c3 prevents this."

Figure 106. After a flurry of moves and exchanges, the board looked like this. Neither player could win undisputed control of the open file.

"Well, that was a lot of trouble for nothing," grumbled Gary. "Why all the fuss about moving your Rook onto an open file if there is no possibility of a back-rank checkmate?"

Enemy Rook on the 7th (or 2d) Rank

"Even if it does not produce a back-rank checkmate, a Rook on an open file can do considerable damage by moving onto the 7th rank if it is a White Rook (or onto the 2d rank if Black). To illustrate I will set up the board with a White Rook in control of an open file." Having said this, Sammy arranged the board as in Figure 107A, and he then asked, "How should WHITE move if it is WHITE's turn to move?"

"Again, after what you just said, that is obvious," replied Joan. "By moving 1. Rd1-d7, WHITE places a Rook on the 7th rank." After Joan made the move (Fig. 107B), Sammy said,

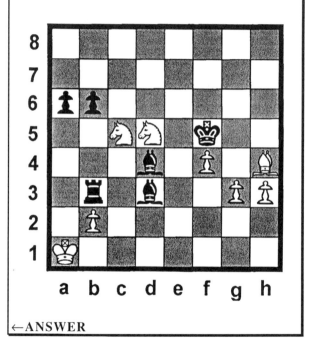

QUIZ—(a) What is WHITE's best move if it is WHITE's move?
(b) What is BLACK's move if it is BLACK's move instead of WHITE's?

←ANSWER

(a) Nd5-e7+, mate; (b) ...Rb3-a3+, mate.

160

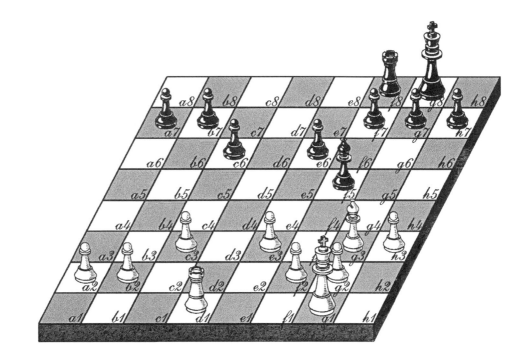

Figure 107A. The White Rook has full control of the d file. What should WHITE's next move be?

"Good, the White Rook now attacks the Black Pawn on b7 and there is very little BLACK can do about it."

Gary asked, "Why can't BLACK move 1. ...Rf8-b8 to protect the b7 Pawn with the Black Rook?" Sammy let Gary make the move (Fig. 107B) but then said, "Not good. The White Bishop on g3 would then capture the Black Rook. A better move might be 1. ...b7-b5."

"But now," protested Stella, "the White Rook

Figure 107B. Bad news for BLACK. The White Rook has moved onto the 7th rank.

will capture the Black Pawn on a7."

"That's true," said Sammy, "but there is little else BLACK can do. That White Rook on the 7th rank is causing real problems and, as is often the case, is threatening all the Black Pawns on this rank. BLACK will be lucky to lose only this one Pawn."

Doubled Rooks

"Even better than having *one* Rook on an open file is to have *two* Rooks on it. When two friendly Rooks occupy the same file or rank, and there are no chessmen between them, each protects the other. This powerful self-protective combination, called a **doubled Rook**, can put even the enemy Queen to flight. I saw the two workmen replaying the same moves that were played in London in 1922. It was in a game between Alexander Alekhine (playing WHITE) and F.D. Yates (BLACK). Alekhine, who held the world championship from 1927 to 1935 and again in 1937, was well on his way to beating Yates after nineteen moves." Sammy had the remarkable memory of an International Grand Master and set up the board as it looked in the 1922 Alekhine-Yates match after BLACK had moved 19. ...b5-b4 (Fig. 108A).

"You will note," Sammy continued, "that the White Rook has uncontested control of the open c file. Although the game continued for 19 more moves, after all Yates (BLACK) was also a grand master, WHITE's next move was the beginning of the end for BLACK. Can you tell me what your next move would be if you were WHITE?"

Gary and Cary swam in lazy circles studying the board below them. Joan and Stella scuttled around it to study it from WHITE's viewpoint. Joan, who seemed to be the star of the class,

Figure 108A. After 19 moves during the 1922 match between Alekhine (WHITE) and Yates (BLACK) the board looked like this. BLACK had just moved 19. ...b5-b4. WHITE was now about to make a very strong move. Can you see it?

said, "WHITE should move 20. Rf1-c1." Since Sammy did not say 'no,' she made the move (Fig. 108B).

"Marvelous, that is just what Alekhine did." said Sammy. "Look what that move does. WHITE has a doubled Rook on the c file. This open file, as often happens, now becomes a breakthrough path for WHITE's army to penetrate deep into BLACK's territory. After several more moves, WHITE (Alekhine) had achieved the following

Figure 108B. After 19. ...b5-b4, WHITE moved 20. Rf1-c1 and now had two Rooks (doubled Rooks) on the open c file. This was really bad news for BLACK.

position." Sammy then set up the board as in Figure 109.

"Wow!" exclaimed Gary. "WHITE has doubled Rooks on the 7th rank!"

"Yes," said Sammy, "the doubled Rooks on the 7th rank practically have a stranglehold on BLACK's King. After a few more moves, BLACK resigned.

"The International Grand Master, Yasser Seirawan, refers to doubled Rooks on the 7th rank as 'pigs on the 7th.' That is because they are almost unstoppable and gobble up (capture)

Figure 109. After a few more moves in the Alekhine-Yates match, WHITE, as shown here, had achieved a chessplayer's dream—doubled Rooks on an opponent's next-to-last rank. The threat to BLACK's King is overpowering and, after a few more moves, BLACK resigned.

one Black chessman after the other. And you have already seen how tightly they imprison BLACK's King."

OTHER COOPERATIONS

Cary Grunt, having in mind the previous day's discussion of open files and doubled Rooks, began the morning lesson by asking, "Are doubled Rooks the only examples where two chesspieces, each protecting the other, cooperate and sometimes deliver a long-range punch?"

"No," replied Sammy, "there are other cooperative combinations, but these involve the Queen. Such combinations may involve the Queen and a Rook, a Queen and a Bishop, and even a Queen and two Rooks. I'll set up the board to show you some examples."

6. Ne4-d6+, mate. WHITE now checks BLACK's King, and the Pawn on e6 cannot capture this Knight. Why?

KNOCK-OUT PUNCH—In 1935 Alexander Alekhine, world champion from 1927-1935 and 1937-1945, played against four players.

WHITE (Alekhine)   BLACK (the Allies)
1.   e2-e4   c7-c6
2.   d2-d4   d7-d5
3.   Nb1-c3   d5xe4
4.   Nc3xe4   Nb8-d7
5.   Qd1-e2   Ng8-f6??

The board now looked as shown below. What was WHITE's next move?

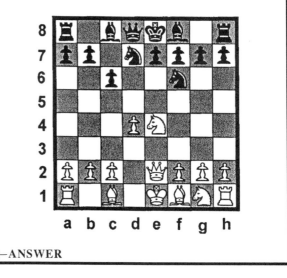

←ANSWER

167

Queen and Rook

"Because the Queen can move like a Rook," Sammy continued, "she and one of her Rooks can act like a doubled Rook. The Queen may be at the front end or the back end of the battering ram they form. I'll set up the board with her at the front end (Fig. 110A). How can WHITE use this battering ram?"

Joan replied almost immediately. "The White Queen by moving 1. Qg4xg7 can batter into BLACK's castle to capture the Pawn and checkmate BLACK's King."

Figure 110A. WHITE's Queen and Rook combination protect each other to form a battering ram to attack BLACK's castle. How should WHITE move if it is WHITE's move? If it is BLACK's move, note that ...g7-g6 defends against WHITE's Queen-Rook battering ram.

"Precisely," said Sammy. "And now I'll set up the board with the White Queen and her two Rooks lined up on an open file (Fig. 110B). Now *that* is a powerful battering ram. Can you see how WHITE can use it?"

"Yes, indeed," replied Stella, "WHITE smashes onto the 8th Rank to check BLACK's King by 1. Re5xe8+. BLACK's best possible reply is 1. ...Rb8xe8, but now WHITE moves 2. Qe3xe8+. BLACK then moves 2. ...Qc6xe8 to capture WHITE's Queen, but then WHITE's Rook captures the Black Queen by 3. Re1xe8+ and thus checkmates BLACK.

Figure 110B. WHITE's overpowering battering ram on the e file can bring about a checkmate of BLACK. WHITE begins with 1. Re5xe8+.

Queen and Bishop

"Sometimes the Queen and one of her Bishops line up on the same diagonal to form a battering ram that operates along the Bishop's diagonal. This, too, is a long-range battering ram that can, given the chance, penetrate deep into enemy territory." Having said that, Sammy set up the board as in Figure 111 and then asked, "If it's BLACK's move, what move is best?" It did not take long for Joan to say, "With just one move, BLACK can checkmate WHITE." Sammy turned to the others and asked, "Do you see it,

Figure 111. BLACK's Bishop and Queen also form a battering ram. If it is BLACK's move, how should BLACK move? If it is WHITE's move instead, do you see how WHITE can checkmate BLACK in two moves?

170

too?" Stella scurried around the board studying it intently as Cary and Gary swam in place above it. Then she said, "Yes, I see it. BLACK should move ...Qb5-f1, checkmate." "Of course," agreed Gary.

TOUCH-MOVE

"Sammy, Sammy, Sammy," Cary said in his debonair way. "Don't you think it is high time for us to start playing actual chess games with each other?"

"Well, replied Sammy, "you still need to know more. For example, do you know that if you touch one of your own chessmen, you *must* move it, if it has a legal move? And that if you touch an enemy chessman, you must capture it, if possible? In friendly games the touch-move rule may be relaxed, but in matches and tournaments it is always strictly enforced."

"But what if one of my chessmen is not located on the center of its square and I want to adjust it to be better centered?" asked Stella.

"In that case," Sammy said, "you first say **j'adoube** which is French for 'I adjust.' Having said that, you are allowed to position your chessman better on its square."

During the 1970 Matulovic-Bilek match, Matulovic made a move, saw that it lost the game, and quickly said, "J'adoube." He then took back the move! This was illegal—you must say "J'adoube" BEFORE you touch a misplaced chessman. But Bilek was so dumbfounded that he failed to protest. Matulovic eventually won, but the spectators subsequently called him "J'adoubovic."
From *The World of Chess* by Saidy and Lessing

THE DEVIL AND CAPABLANCA

"That reminds me of a story I heard the one attendant tell the other. Of course, it is not a true story. It was in a book of chess stories he had read and concerned the Cuban chessmaster José Capablanca (1888-1942). In 1921 Capablanca became world champion and was considered unbeatable. He required anyone who wanted to challenge him to put up a stake of $10,000 in gold. That was a lot of money, so most of the world's top players hesitated to challenge him. In

1927, however, Alexander Alekhine (1892-1946) found some people to put up the money and challenged Capablanca. Alekhine, who was born in Moscow but later lived in Paris, defeated Capablanca (six wins, three losses, and 25 draws).

"All that is true, but now comes the fiction. After his defeat, Capablanca returned to his home in Havana. And one day, as the story goes, a dark-haired stranger, dressed all in black, knocked on his door and challenged Capablanca to a game of chess. Capablanca was disdainful and said he just did not play against any 'woodpusher' who showed up. (Most of the chessmen used by beginners in those days were made of wood.) The dark stranger said he was by no means a weak player. Indeed, he said he was from the school of players associated with Alekhine. Smarting from his defeat by Alekhine,

Capablanca invited the stranger in and asked what stakes they should play for. The stranger said, 'Let us play the game and the winner can ask anything he wants from the loser.' Those were high stakes, indeed, but Capablanca, in his confidence, agreed to them. As the game progressed, the stranger proved to be a very strong player, stronger even than Capablanca. It soon became apparent that he would defeat Capablanca. With some relish, the stranger asked Capablanca, 'Do you know who I am?' By this time Capablanca suspected that he was playing against the Devil and that if the Devil won, Capablanca would lose his soul. But he answered, 'No.' The stranger then said, 'I am Satan.' Capablanca replied, 'I don't believe it. Prove it.' 'How do you want me to prove it?' asked the stranger. And Capablanca replied 'Touch this flower and turn it to gold.' So the

Devil touched a flower on the mantle and turned it to gold. Capablanca said, 'Touch this chessman and turn it to gold.' So the Devil did. And now Capablanca claimed, 'It's your move and you touched your man. Now you have to move it.' And because Satan had to move that particular piece, it turned his sure win into a draw. In a puff of sulfurous smoke, he vanished from Capablanca's house."

COMMONLY USED OPENINGS

Cary's impatience to start playing actual games was shared by Joan. "That was a very amusing story," she said rather dryly, which is hard to do if you live in an aquarium. And then she almost sighed, "Aren't we ready to play now?"

"Just about," said Sammy, "but first you will need to know some of the moves commonly used to begin a game. These sets of moves are called **openings**, and entire books have been written on chess openings. We are only going to 'scratch the surface' for four different openings: The Ruy Lopez; The Giuoco Piano; The Sicilian Defense; and The Queen's Gambit Declined."

"Say," said Stella, "haven't we already discussed the Ruy Lopez opening?"

"Yes," Sammy replied, "we did in an early lesson. But it is such an important opening that we should review it and discuss it in greater detail."

The Ruy Lopez Opening

Although the Spanish priest, Ruy Lopez, described this opening over 430 years ago, it remains a highly respected, much used opening even today. It is a strong opening for WHITE that rapidly develops WHITE's Kings'-side pieces.

Even after you become experienced players, it likely will be the opening you will prefer." Sammy continued by saying, "Up to BLACK's second move, the moves are:

	WHITE	BLACK
1.	e2-e4	e7-e5
2.	Ng1-f3	

As you can see (Fig. 112A), both players have advanced their e-Pawns to begin the fight for control of the center. And then WHITE moved 2. Ng1-f3. As I asked earlier (p. 51), 'Why move 2. Ng1-f3?'"

Figure 112A. Sammy reviews the first few moves of the Ruy Lopez Opening. Both players fight for control of the center.

After studying the board, Joan replied, "The White Knight when on f3 attacks BLACK's Pawn on e5 and also exerts pressure on center square d4."

"What else?" asked Sammy.

Gary Grouper then replied, "The move 2. Ng1-f3 develops the White Knight off the back rank and helps bring WHITE one step closer to being able to castle."

Figure 112B. The next few moves of the Ruy Lopez Opening.

Sammy now made BLACK's second move, 2. ...Nb8-c6, and WHITE's third, 3. Bf1-b5 for the Ruy Lopez (Fig. 112B). He then asked, "Why did BLACK reply 2. ...Nb8-c6?"

Stella answered, "This develops the Black

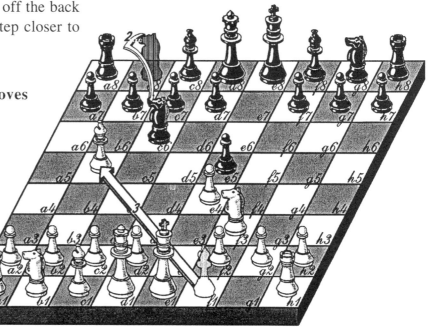

Knight off BLACK's back rank *and at the same time* protects the Black Pawn on e5. Also, the Black Knight fights the White Knight for control of center square d4."

"Good," said Sammy, "but why does WHITE now move 3. Bf1-b5?"

No one answered Sammy's last question, so he answered it himself. "With the White Bishop on b5, BLACK would hesitate to advance the Black d-Pawn. Why?"

Joan replied, "If BLACK advances the d-Pawn, by say, d7-d6, the White Bishop on d5 will be pinning the Black Knight against the Black King."

"Exactly," said Sammy, "and BLACK prefers that this should not happen. As a result the next moves of the Ruy Lopez are:

	WHITE	BLACK
3.	...	a7-a6
4.	Bb5-a4	Ng8-f6."

Sammy showed these moves on the board (Fig. 113A) and then continued, "As you can see, by moving 3. ...a7-a6, BLACK attacks the White Bishop with a Pawn, so the Bishop retreats by 4. Bb5-a4. BLACK could now move 4. ...b7-b5 to attack the White Bishop with the Black b-Pawn. This might be a good move for beginning players, but skilled players usually delay this move and instead move 4. ...Ng8-f6. Why?"

The four students studied the board (Fig. 113A), and Stella replied, "BLACK develops the Black Knight and, at the same time, attacks the White Pawn on e4. Also, the Black Knight exerts pressure on center square d5."

"Precisely," said Sammy. "That is an excellent move for BLACK."

Sammy then continued by showing them the fifth moves of the Ruy Lopez opening (Fig. 113B).

| 5. | 0-0 | Bf8-e7 |

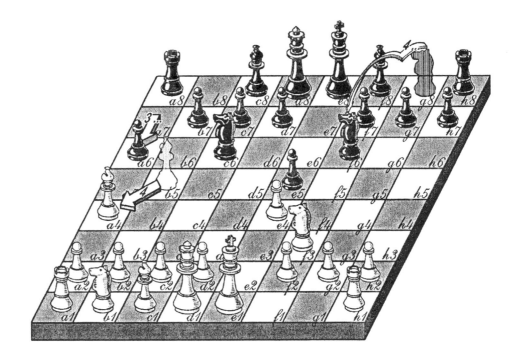

Figure 113A. A few more moves for the Ruy Lopez Opening.
With 3. ...a7-a6 BLACK forces the White Bishop to retreat (4. Bb5-a4).
BLACK then moves 4. ...Ng8-f6.

Figure 113B. The fifth moves of the Ruy Lopez Opening. WHITE castles 5. 0-0, and BLACK prepares to castle by moving 5. ...Bf8-e7.

and explained, "WHITE's Kings'-side castling gets the White King into a protective pocket and, at the same time, gets the White Rook into the battle. And then BLACK moves 5. ...Bf8-e7."

"Wait a minute," said Joan, "why does BLACK move 5. ...Bf8-e7? Why not move 5. ...Nf6xe4?"

"Good question," answered Sammy, "that move does look like it will win a Pawn for BLACK. But it won't, because WHITE will win back a pawn by moving 6. Rf1-e1. The White Rook will now skewer BLACK's Knight and Pawn. If BLACK defends the Knight by d7-d5 or f7-f5, the Black King will be exposed to great danger. So BLACK would have to move the Knight and permit WHITE to move Nf3xe5 to capture the Black Pawn. That's why BLACK, instead of snatching a Pawn by 5. ...Nf6xe4, instead moves 5. ...Bf8-e7. This gets BLACK ready to castle Kings' side.

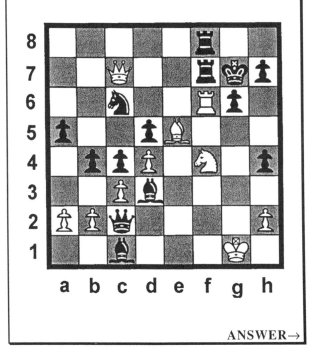

QUIZ—(a) What is WHITE's best move?
(b) If it is BLACK's move, how should BLACK move?

ANSWER→

179

"The next moves of the Ruy Lopez, as I will demonstrate (Fig. 113C), are

	WHITE	BLACK
6.	Rf1-e1	b7-b5

By 6. Rf1-e1, WHITE directs the White Rook's fire power along the e-file. And by 6. ...b7-b5, BLACK finally drives off the pesky White Bishop to free up the Black d-Pawn."

Figure 113C. The sixth moves of the Ruy Lopez.

The Giuoco Piano Opening

"Italian chess players developed the Giuoco Piano during the 15th century. It is a good opening for beginners, but it is rarely used in tournaments between advanced players because it lacks the 'zing' of the Ruy Lopez. Indeed, *giuoco piano* (pronounced 'jocko pee-on-oh')

means 'quiet game' in Italian. Its first three moves (Fig. 114A) are:

	WHITE	BLACK
1.	e2-e4	e7-e5
2.	Ng1-f3	Nb8-c6
3.	Bf1-c4	Bf8-c5

Figure 114A. For the Giuoco Piano Opening, the first two moves are the same as for the Ruy Lopez. On the third move, however, WHITE moves 3. Bf1-c4 instead of the more audacious 3. Bf1-b5 of the Ruy Lopez. This produces a more easygoing game.

On their fourth moves

	WHITE	BLACK
4.	Nb1-c3	Ng8-f6

each player develops his or her remaining Knight so that the board looks like this (Fig. 114B). Each player is now ready to castle kings' side."

"So you recommend that we use the Giuoco Piano Opening?" asked Gary.

"Yes." said Sammy, "For beginners it is less complicated than the Ruy Lopez, which should be the next opening you try. However, I am now going to demonstrate two more openings."

Figure 114B. The Giuoco Piano Opening after the first four moves.

182

Queen's Gambit Declined

"In the previous openings, WHITE began with 1. e2-e4. In the old days this was called a King's Pawn opening because the e-Pawns, being located in front of the Kings, were called King's Pawns."

Joan now interrupted Sammy to ask "Were the Pawns in front of the Queens called Queen's Pawns?"

"Precisely." said Sammy. "Even today the d-Pawns are sometimes called Queen's Pawns and the e-Pawns are sometimes called King's Pawns."

Sammy continued, "Upon occasion WHITE may begin a game by 1. d2-d4, thus advancing the Queen's Pawn. BLACK's usual reply is 1. ...d7-d5 and the two Queen's Pawns blockade each other. And now WHITE moves 2. c2-c4. I will set up the board to show these moves" (Fig. 115).

FIANCHETTO—A strategy in chess where a b- or g-Pawn is advanced one square, and its Bishop later moves onto the square thus vacated. The Bishop is then said to be "fianchettoed" and from its snug location trains its firepower along one or the other of the board's longest diagonals—a1-h8 or a8-h1.

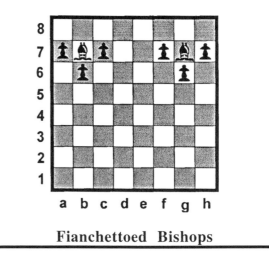

Fianchettoed Bishops

"Wow!" said Cary, "WHITE is offering BLACK a free Pawn!"

"So it seems," replied Sammy, "and as you may recall, such offers of free material are called gambits. This offer of WHITE's c-Pawn is called the Queen's Gambit."

"Shouldn't BLACK grab that free Pawn?" asked Cary.

"No," said Sammy, "that is just what WHITE wants. WHITE hopes to trade material, in this case

Figure 115. The Queen's Gambit.

his or her c-Pawn, for a positional advantage—namely, the deflection of BLACK's Queen's Pawn away from the center. If BLACK takes the Pawn by 2. ...d5xc4, WHITE will easily capture the Black Pawn (now on c4) by moving 3. Qd1-a4+. Now the White Queen forks this Pawn and BLACK's King. After BLACK moves to defend the King, WHITE's Queen will capture the Pawn. And later WHITE can move 3. e2-e4 to achieve an absolute stranglehold on the center."

"So, instead of capturing WHITE's c-Pawn (= Queen's Gambit Accepted), BLACK usually declines to capture it (= Queen's Gambit Declined) and may move either 2. ...e7-e6 (= Orthodox Defense) or 2. ...c7-c6 (Slav Defense). By use of the Slav Defense, BLACK puts up a good fight for control of the four center squares."

U.S. CHESS HALL OF FAME & MUSEUM—U.S. Chess Center [1501 M St., NW, Washington, DC 20005: (202) 857-4922] is home to chess classes and this free museum.

FEDERATIONS, CLUBS, AND RATINGS—A gold mine of chess information is available from the United States Chess Federation [186 Route 9W, New Windsor, NY 12553: (800) 388-5464]. USCF membership (1 year: $15 if under 20; $40 if 20-64; $30 if 65 or over) will bring, each month, a copy of *Chess Life*. For under 20's, a Scholastic USCF membership ($10 per year) will bring the bimonthly *School Mates* instead of *Chess Life*. By participating in USCF-sponsored chess tournaments, members will receive national chess ratings. Guidepost values: Beginners, 900s; State Champions, 2300s; World Champion, 2800. In 1994 only four of the USCF's 42,000 members had ratings above 2700. The 20-year-old Gata Kamsky ranks first (at 2762) and may be the first U.S. contender for the world chess crown since Bobby Fischer. Ratings result from entering USCF RATED BEGINNERS OPENS, which are limited to unrated players and those rated below 1200.

The Sicilian Defense (Dragon Variation)

All the fish were eager to play each other, but Sammy asked them to wait until he taught them one more opening, the Sicilian Defense. Reluctantly, they agreed, so Sammy began by saying, "The Sicilian Defense is a cunning defense greatly favored by master chess players when they play as BLACK. In their hands, the Sicilian Defense may allow BLACK to gradually overcome the disadvantage of not moving first." Having said this, Sammy set up the board to demonstrate the first few moves of the Sicilian Defense (Fig. 116) and explained, "After WHITE's standard opening move, 1. e2-e4, BLACK cunningly moves 1. ...c7-c5." Joan gasped and said, "Why

would BLACK do that? Has BLACK given up the fight to control the four center squares?"

"Not at all," replied Sammy, "the Black Pawn on c5 slyly attacks square d4 *from the side*. To offset this, WHITE moves 2. Ng1-f3 so that the White Knight's power bears down on squares d4 and e5 (Fig. 116). And now BLACK moves 2. ...d7-d6 to permit the Black Bishop on c8 to train its firepower along the c8-h3 diagonal.

"Incidentally," Sammy added, "many chess champions favor this second move for BLACK, among them the American, Bobby Fischer (1943-), the world champion in 1972. A second advantage of the move is that if WHITE advances the e-Pawn by 3. e4-e5, the Black Pawn on d6 can capture it. Actually, WHITE usually moves 3. d2-d4 (Fig. 116), and BLACK then moves 3. ...c5xd4, happily trading the c-Pawn for WHITE's better-located d-Pawn. WHITE completes the trade by moving 4. Nf3xd4."

Figure 116. The first moves in the
Sicilian Defense are:

    1. e2-e4   c7-c5

    2. Ng1-f3   d7-d6

    3. d2-d4

The next moves (not shown) are
3. ...c5xd4 and 4. Nf3xd4.

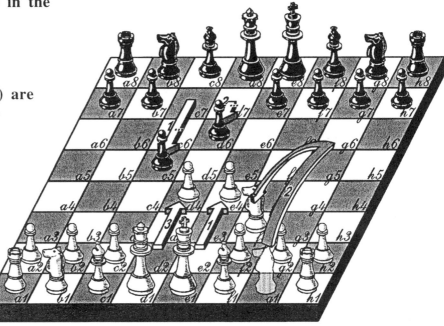

"The battle rages on," Sammy continued, "as BLACK (Fig. 117A) moves 4. ...Ng8-f6 to attack WHITE's e-Pawn. WHITE defends this Pawn by moving 5. Nb1-c3, and BLACK replies 5. ...g7-g6. At this point BLACK's Pawns are located where you see them (Fig. 117A), and some fancy that they resemble the outline of a dragon. Maybe so, but personally, I cannot see this at all. Be that as it may, this version of the Sicilian Defense has been called the Dragon variation because of this fancied outline. After BLACK moves 5. ...g7-g6, WHITE moves 6. Bc1-e3 to develop this Bishop. And now BLACK moves 6. ...Bf8-g7 (Fig. 117B). Can you see what BLACK has accomplished?

Stella answered, "BLACK has fianchettoed the Bishop and, at the same time, prepares to castle on the King's side."

"Precisely," Sammy gurgled excitedly, "and the fianchettoed Bishop can now direct its firepower along h8-a1, one of the board's two longest diagonals.

"Well," Sammy reflected, "the Sicilian Defense is perhaps too complicated for beginners. So Maybe we should move on."

Joan now broke in to say, "I'm for that. Indeed, we now know how the chessmen move and we know some of the standard openings. Why can't we begin to play each other?"

Sammy knew his students had a lot more to learn, but he also knew they had to start sometime. Besides, the only way to truly learn chess is to play. So he said, "Why not? Let's play."

And so began the first chess tournament ever held between unrated fish.

Figure 117A. After 3. ...c5xd4 and 4. Nf3xd4, the Sicilian Defense continues with:

    4. ...   Ng8-f6

    5. Nb1-c3   g7-g6

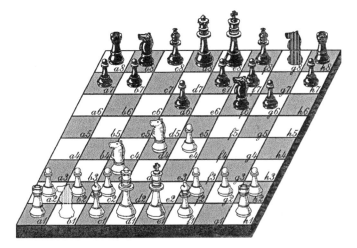

Figure 117B. And with:

    6. Bc1-e3   Bf8-g7

APPENDIX: THE LAWS OF CHESS

The World Chess Federation or, as it is known in French, the *Fédération Internationale des Echecs*, is familiarly referred to by chess players as *F.I.D.E.*, or *FIDE*. The official American translation of the laws of chess adopted by *FIDE* was made by its American representative, the United States Chess Federation [186 Route 9W, New Windsor, New York, NY 12553]. The gist of many of these laws—in particular, those describing the moves of the men—has already been given and, hence, need not be repeated. However, the reader should also be familiar with the laws governing a touched man, the completion of a move, and the instances wherein draws may be claimed. These laws, abstracted from the official American translation of *FIDE*'s laws, are therefore appended. Better yet, read the *Official Rules of Chess* (purchasable from the USCF).

The Touched Man

In case some chessman is badly off center on its square, the player having the move, *provided that he first warns his opponent*, may adjust one or more men on their squares. In any other case, if the player having the move touches one or more of his own men, he must move the first man touched, or if it has no legal moves, the second man touched, etc. The rule in chess is: *Touch—move*. If the player having the move touches one of his opponent's men, he must capture it, if this is legally possible. The player who touches a man is not forced to obey these laws unless his opponent, before he begins his own move by touching a man, points out the violation and requires such penalty. No penalty can be exacted if a player touches one of his own men that cannot be legally moved or he touches one of his opponent's men but cannot legally capture it.

Completion of a Move

A move transferring a man to a vacant square is officially complete when the player releases the man on the new square. A move involving a capture is complete after the captured man has been removed and the player has placed and released his own man on the square formerly occupied by the captured man. In castling, the move is completed once the player has released the Rook on the square crossed by the King. *It is important to note that in castling, the King should be moved first.* Once the King has been moved two squares over and released, the player has no right to make any other move than castling.

In the promotion of a Pawn, the move is complete only after the player releases the new man that he has selected to replace his Pawn.

Drawn Games

A game is drawn:

1. If a King is stalemated.

2. If both players agree to a draw.

3. By a player, if he or she is able to force moves such that the chessmen occur in the same positions on the board at least three times (see Fig. 88). A perpetual check (Fig. 89) also results in a drawn game.

4. If the player having the move demonstrates—and it will be necessary to have recorded all the moves of the game to do this—that at least 50 moves have been made by each side without a Pawn being moved or a chessman captured. The number of moves may be increased beyond 50 only by agreement prior to the beginning of the game.

INDEX